DIVERSITY OF LIFE
RESOURCES

IMAGES, DATA, AND READINGS

DEVELOPED AT LAWRENCE HALL OF SCIENCE, UNIVERSITY OF CALIFORNIA AT BERKELEY
PUBLISHED AND DISTRIBUTED BY DELTA EDUCATION

FOSS Middle School Curriculum Development Team

Linda De Lucchi, Larry Malone, Co-Directors; **Dr. Lawrence F. Lowery,** Principal Investigator
Dr. Terry Shaw, Teri Dannenberg, Dr. Susan Brady, Susan Kaschner Jagoda, Curriculum Developers
Dr. Kathy Long, Assessment Coordinator
Carol Sevilla, Graphic Designer; **Rose Craig,** Illustrator
Anne Marie Gearhart, Surendra Ambegaokar, Database Assistants
Alev Burton, Administrative Support; **Mark Warren,** Equipment Manager

ScienceVIEW Multimedia Design Team

Dr. Marco Molinaro, Director
Dr. Susan Ketchner, Producer; **Rebecca Shapley,** Revision Producer
Leigh Anne McConnaughey, Principal Illustrator and Producer; **Wolf Read,** Senior Illustrator
Dan Bluestein, Revision Programmer; **Ward Ryan,** Lead Programmer; **Roger Vang,** Programmer
Guillaume Brasseur, Computer Administrator, Video Editor, Vocals, and QA Manager
Alicia Nieves, Quality Assurance; **Theresa Slaman,** Administrative Support

Special Contributors

Pam Pelletier, Content Specialist, Northeastern University
Anthony Cody, Teacher; **Denise Soderlund,** Teacher; **Tarren Shaw,** Consultant
Marshall Montgomery, Materials Design; **Silven Read,** Lab Technician
Alicia Cordero, Biologist/Consultant; **Dr. Rob Guralnick,** Biologist/Consultant
Wai Pang Chan, UCB Scientific Visualization Center; **Rick Staples,** Technical Instrument, San Francisco
Professors Tom Bruns and **John Taylor,** Department of Plant and Microbial Biology, UC Berkeley
Dr. Michael S. Caterino, Essig Museum of Entomology, UC Berkeley
Adrian Barnett, Akodon Ecological Consulting
Rockman ET AL., Evaluators

Delta Education FOSS Middle School Team

Bonnie Piotrowski, FOSS Managing Editor; **Mathew Bacon, Grant Gardner, Tom Guetling, Joann Hoy,
Dana Koch, Cathrine Monson, John Prescott, Paul Scopa, Dave Vissoe**

National Trial Teachers

Mary McGinnis, Barnard White M. S., Union City, CA; **Karen Lane,** Bluford Grade School, Bluford, IL
Jacque Thomas, Bluford Grade School, Bluford, IL; **Julie McKinney,** Hudson H. S., Hudson, MA
Sarah Chapin, Hudson H. S., Hudson, MA; **Gayle Dunlap,** Walter T. Bergen M. S., Bloomingdale, NJ
Donna Moran, Walter T. Bergen M. S., Bloomingdale, NJ; **Joan Caroselli,** J. E. Soehl M. S., Linden, NJ
John Kuzma, McManus M. S., Linden, NJ; **Susan Reed,** Irving M. S., Norman, OK
David Jacks, Irving M. S., Norman, OK; **Melissa Gibbons,** Dunbar M. S., Fort Worth, TX
Cheryl Berhane, Reeves M. S., Olympia, WA; **Virginia Reid,** Thurgood Marshall M. S., Olympia, WA

FOSS for Middle School Project
Lawrence Hall of Science, University of California
Berkeley, CA 94720 510-642-8941

Delta Education
P.O. Box 3000 80 Northwest Blvd.
Nashua, NH 03063 1-800-258-1302

The FOSS Middle School Program was developed in part with the support of the National Science Foundation Grant ESI 9553600. However, any opinions, findings, conclusions, statements, and recommendations expressed herein are those of the authors and do not necessarily reflect the views of the NSF.

Diversity of Life

Contents

Contents

Images

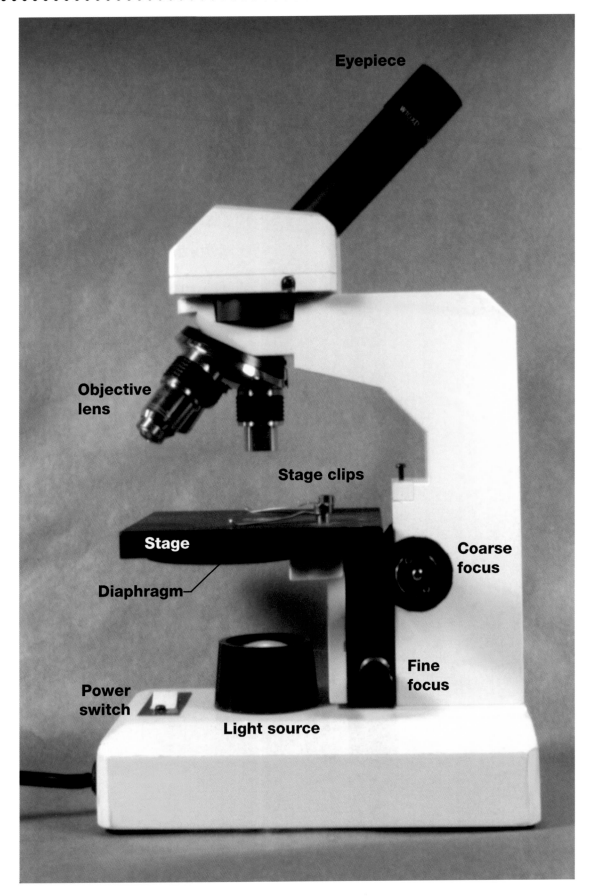

Eyepiece

Objective lens

Stage clips

Stage

Diaphragm

Coarse focus

Fine focus

Power switch

Light source

MICROORGANISM GUIDE
GREEN ALGAE

1.

2.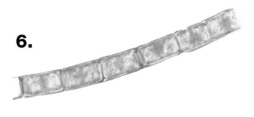

3.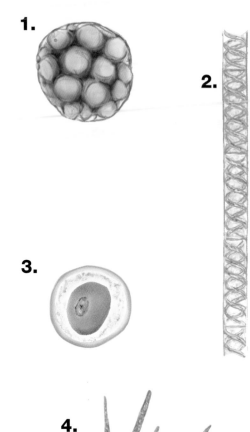

4.

5.

6.

7.

1. *Coelastrum*

2. *Spirogyra*

3. *Protococcus*

4. *Cladophora*

5. *Hydrodictyon*

6. *Microspora*

7. *Oedogonium*

MICROORGANISM GUIDE
CILIATES

1.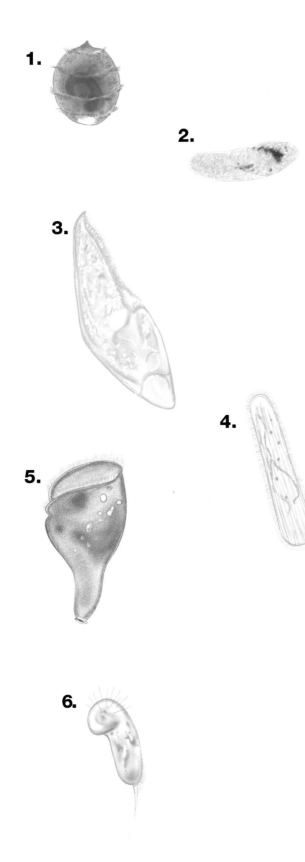

2.

3.

4.

5.

6.

7.

8.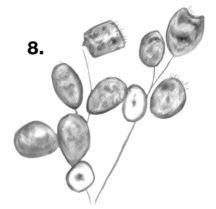

1. *Didinium*

2. *Paramecium*

3. *Blepharisma*

4. *Spirostomum*

5. *Stentor*

6. *Euplotes*

7. *Vorticella*

8. *Zoothamnium*

MICROORGANISM GUIDE
FLAGELLATES AND SARCODINES

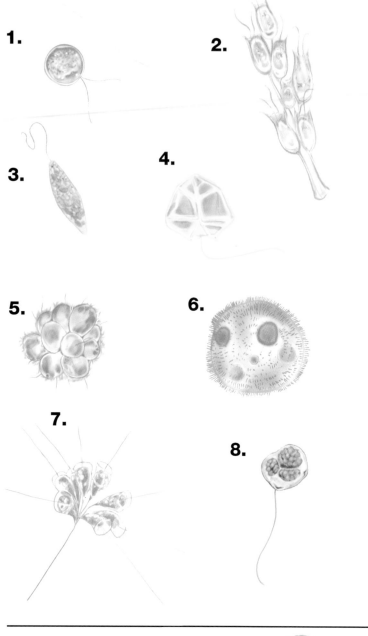

Flagellates

1. *Chlamydomonas*

2. *Dinobryon*

3. *Euglena*

4. *Peridinium*

5. *Synura*

6. *Volvox*

7. *Codosiga*

8. *Oikomonas*

9. *Bodo*

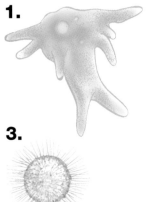

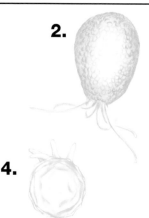

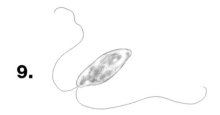

Sarcodines

1. *Amoeba*

2. *Difflugia*

3. *Actinosphaerium*

4. *Arcella*

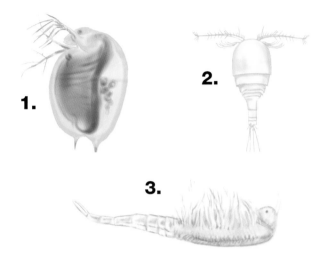

Crustaceans

1. *Daphnia*

2. Copepods

3. Fairy shrimp

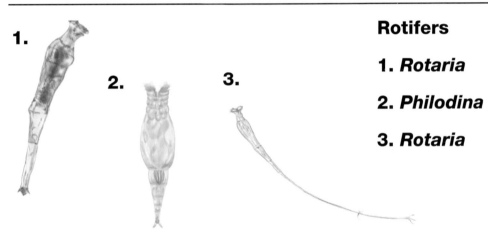

Rotifers

1. *Rotaria*

2. *Philodina*

3. *Rotaria*

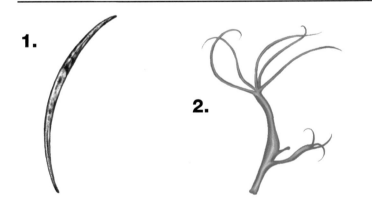

Others

1. Nematode

2. *Hydra*

3. Tardigrade

CELL SIZE COMPARISON

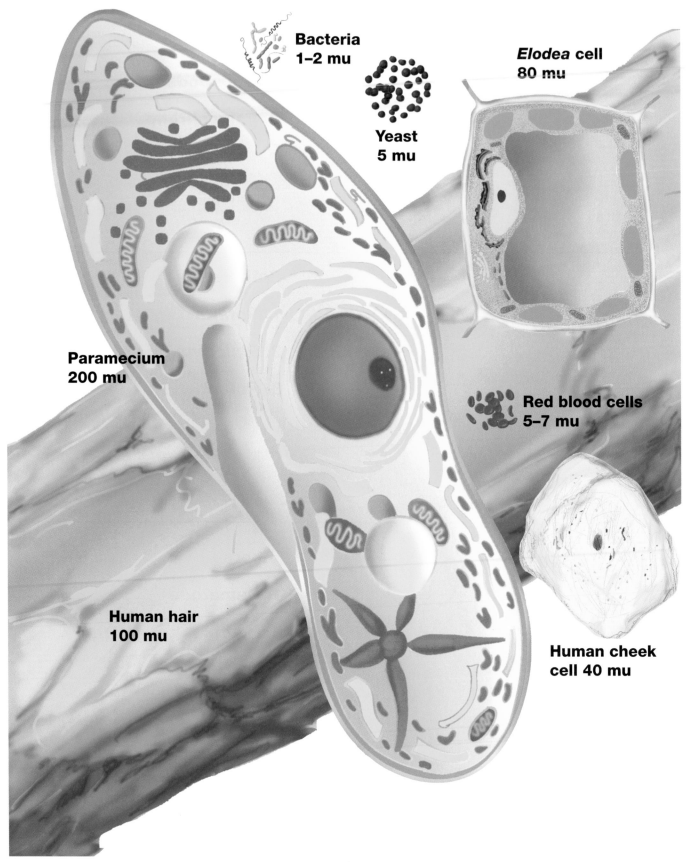

Bacteria
1–2 mu

Yeast
5 mu

Elodea cell
80 mu

Paramecium
200 mu

Red blood cells
5–7 mu

Human hair
100 mu

Human cheek
cell 40 mu

How BIG Are Cells?

As a rule, cells are small. The illustration on the facing page shows the relative size of several cells that you might have seen. They are illustrated with a typical strand of human hair in the background for size comparison. As you can see, most cells are smaller than the diameter of a hair.

The sizes of the cells are indicated in units called microns (mu). Remember, a millimeter is one-thousandth of a meter. If you take one millimeter and divide it into one thousand parts, you have divided it into microns. A micron is one-thousandth of a millimeter, or one-millionth of a meter.

A good microscope set at 400x is barely able to resolve objects that are 1 or 2 mu across.

A human hair is on the order of 100 mu in diameter. If you lay 10 hairs side by side they will occupy about a millimeter. It might take 50 or more bacteria to equal the diameter of the hair because bacteria are generally 1–2 micrometers in size. However, some bacteria are significantly smaller—less than 1 micron.

The human cheek cell illustrated is a pretty large human cell at 40–50 microns in diameter. The little red blood cells are 5–7 microns, placing them on the small side of human cells. The majority of the 100 trillion or so cells in a human are in the 20-micron range.

The paramecium is a single-celled organism in the kingdom Protista. Some paramecia can grow as large as 300 microns, gaining them elephant status in their environment. Large as they are, paramecia look tiny compared to the largest cells that have been discovered. A small green marine alga called *Acetabularia* can reach a length of 2 or more centimeters, and it is a single cell! If we were to illustrate it to scale in order to compare it to the cells on page 8, we would need a piece of paper 50 times taller than this one. Imagine placing this illustration on the sidewalk by a four-story building. The *Acetabularia* cell would reach up to the roof.

Cells are generally small to make sure that they are able to conduct the business of life efficiently. Small cells can easily circulate the vital gases and food to all parts of the cell, and quickly move wastes to the cell membrane for removal. If cells were too large, organelles in the middle of the cell would not get the resources they need to continue functioning. This is the main factor limiting cell size.

BESTIARY OF INSECTS

Eastern tailed blue butterfly

Luna moth

Helliconius butterfly

Luna moth caterpillar

Tomato hornworm moth

Chinese oak silk moth

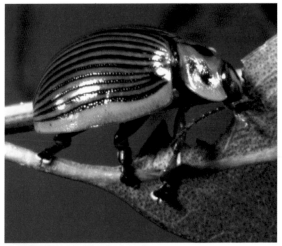

Chrysomelid beetle

Nut weevil

Scarab beetle

Swamp milkweed leaf beetle

Eyed click beetle

Yellow fever mosquito

Housefly

Dragonfly

Milkweed bug

Treehopper thorn mimic

Ant tending aphids

13

Crickets

Grasshopper

Walking stick

Diversity of Life

Data

Contents

Data

TAXONOMIC DESCRIPTION OF LIFE

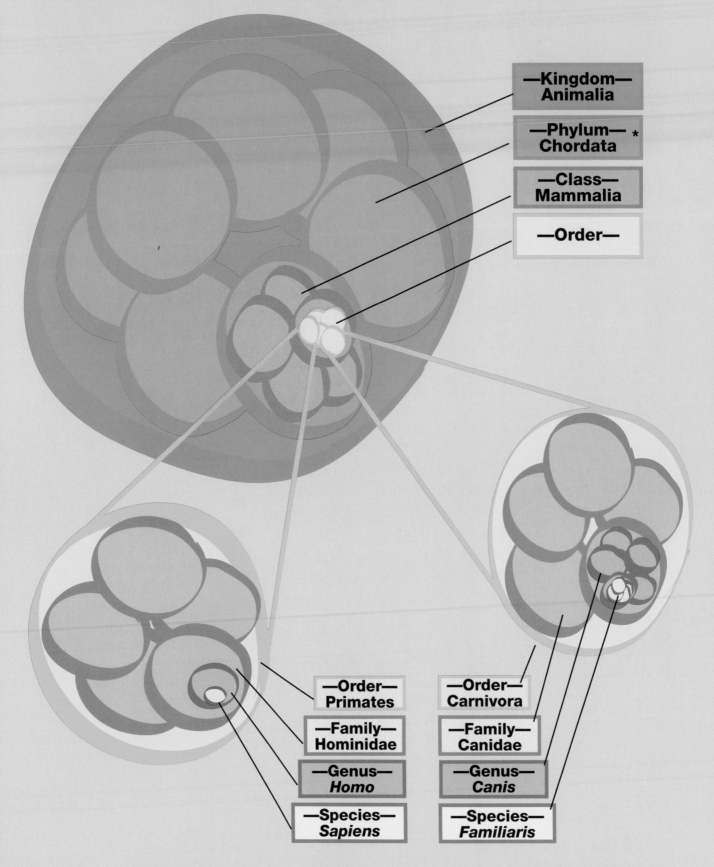

—Kingdom—
Animalia

—Phylum— *
Chordata

—Class—
Mammalia

—Order—

—Order—
Primates

—Family—
Hominidae

—Genus—
Homo

—Species—
Sapiens

—Order—
Carnivora

—Family—
Canidae

—Genus—
Canis

—Species—
Familiaris

* A phylum is called a division in the plant and fungus kingdoms.

Taxonomy

How do scientists organize living organisms? We now know that life is divided into five **kingdoms** based on similarities among the members of each kingdom. The plants all have cell walls and photosynthesize. Animals are multicellular and eat food, and so on. The kingdoms are the grand starting points for organizing life. The five kingdoms are plants, animals, fungi, protists, and monera.

Now what? Each kingdom has thousands of members. The animal kingdom alone has millions of members. There must be ways to further organize them. We know that birds all have feathers and two legs, insects have a hard outer shell and six legs, snakes have no legs, and so on. With a little patience we can sort the animals into some major groups. And then the major groups of animals can be divided further based on some other features. Some birds swim in the water and others don't. Some insects have hard wing covers and others have scales on their wings. Some snakes are poisonous and others are not.

The division of science concerned with the organization of life is **taxonomy.** Taxonomists are continually adding new organisms into the organization as they are discovered and described, and from time to time they rethink the basic organization all together.

The diagram on the facing page shows the current organization of the animal kingdom. The largest circle represents animals. All the known animals are inside the animal-kingdom circle. The aqua circles hold all the animals that share some characteristic. These first subdivisions of the animals are called **phyla** (singular, phylum). One phylum, arthropoda, has all the animals with external skeletons, like crabs, crawdads, and insects. Another phylum has all the flat worms, and another has all the clams and snails. Phylum chordata has all the animals with backbones. We are in phylum chordata, along with the fish, birds, reptiles, amphibians, and the other mammals.

The major subdivisions of a phylum are called **classes.** One class in phylum chordata is mammalia. Mammalia includes all the warm-blooded animals that give live birth (as opposed to laying eggs) and suckle their young. You can probably name dozens of mammals, including animals as diverse as mice, squirrels, apes, raccoons, elephants, seals, tigers, whales, hamsters, and chimps. Humans and dogs are in the same class with all the other mammals.

Mammals are divided into **orders.** This is where humans and dogs split off. Dogs are in order carnivora, along with cats, foxes, weasels, and lots more. Humans are in order primates, along with the monkeys, baboons, lemurs, apes, and chimps. The carnivores and primates are further divided into **families.** All the doglike animals (dogs, wolves, jackals, foxes) are in family canidae, and all the humanlike animals are in family hominidae.

Finally, all the animals that are very similar are collected into the smallest group, the **genus.** Each individual kind of animal in the genus is given a **species** name. Humans are in the genus *Homo,* and have the species name *sapiens.* Animals are known scientifically by their genus and species name. Therefore, you and I are *Homo sapiens.* The genus name is always capitalized, the species name is lowercase, and they are both italicized.

Diversity of Life

Readings

Contents

Readings

LIFE ON EARTH

WHAT IS LIFE?

It's not too difficult to tell that some things are alive. Dogs chasing tennis balls are alive. Birds chattering in a hawthorn tree are alive. Minnows swimming around the plants in a pond are alive. In fact, animals are the first things we learn to recognize as living.

Things that are alive, like the animals described above, are called **organisms.** Any living thing is an organism. But not all organisms are animals. Plants are organisms, too. In the scenes above, the berry tree is alive, and the water plants in the pond are alive.

It's not always so easy to tell that plants are alive, because they don't do some of the things we usually think about when we think about life. Plants don't move around, breathe, eat, or make sounds. Even so, they are alive, and there are ways to figure out that they are alive.

LIVING, DEAD, AND NONLIVING

One way to look at the question What is life? is to think about what makes life come to an end. Every living organism dies after a period of time. An organism is **dead** when it is no longer alive. A fish out of water will die after a short period of time. The fish is still there, it is still made out of the same materials, and it still looks the same as it did when it was living in the water, but it is no longer alive. And this is important—something can only be dead if it once lived. A rock can never be dead because a

21

rock was never alive. We describe the rock as **nonliving.**

Living organisms can be described in terms of two sets of characteristics. One is the **needs** or **requirements** that all organisms have to satisfy to stay alive. The second is the **functions** that all organisms do.

WHAT DO LIVING ORGANISMS NEED?

What do you need to stay alive? It has been said that a person can live 5 minutes without air, 5 days without water, and 5 weeks without food. People need air, water, and food to stay alive.

You breathe air to stay alive. When you breathe in, you bring oxygen into your lungs, where it dissolves into your blood. When you breathe out, carbon dioxide, carbon monoxide, and other waste gases leave your body and go into the air. The process of moving gases into and out of your body is **gas exchange.** Birds do it, bees do it, lizards, fish, baboons, stink bugs, and trees do it. All living organisms engage in gas exchange, and the most common gases involved are oxygen and carbon dioxide.

You drink **water** to stay alive. Even if you don't actually drink pure water, there is water in the fruit, vegetables, soft drinks, milk, and everything else you eat and drink. Water is essential for life as we know it on Earth. It's just that simple: all living organisms need water.

You eat food to stay alive. Food contains energy. Energy is required to make things happen. You can't move, breathe, see, hear, think, or do anything else without energy. All living organisms **use energy** to live.

The process of living produces by-products that are of no use to the organism. In fact, many

by-products are dangerous to the organism if they are allowed to build up. For this reason it is necessary for organisms to get rid of waste products. These might be gases, liquids, or solids. All living organisms **eliminate waste.**

These four basic needs are common to all living organisms: the need for gas exchange, the need for water, the need for energy, and the need to eliminate waste.

WHAT DO LIVING ORGANISMS DO?

Once an organism's basic needs are met, it gets on with the process of life. One of the universal truths is that everything has to be somewhere. That somewhere for an organism is its environment.

People live in towns and go to stores and schools, ride in vehicles, shop, read, watch TV, eat, and millions of other things. The human environment can be colorful and complex. Fish live in oceanic environments, scorpions live in desert environments, maple trees live in forest environments, and so on. When things happen in the environment, organisms respond. All organisms **respond to the environment.**

The ocean fish swims away when the sea lion comes by, the scorpion scurries under a rock when the Sun heats up the ground, and the maple tree's leaves turn red and fall off in the autumn. These are all responses to the environment.

When organisms start life, they are small. As time passes, they get bigger. Increase in size is called growth. The chemical building blocks for growth come from food and from the environment in the form of minerals. All organisms **grow.**

Organisms don't live forever. Some live a short time and some live a long time, but eventually every individual will die. To make sure that the species doesn't become extinct, living organisms make new organisms of their kind. Even though the ways that different kinds of organisms do it vary dramatically, all living organisms **reproduce.** That's not to say every individual organism will reproduce, but every population of organisms reproduces to keep the species going.

All organisms do three things: they respond to the environment, they grow, and they reproduce. Anything that does not have the ability to do all three of these things is not an organism.

There is actually one more characteristic common to all living organisms. That characteristic is not discussed in this article, but will be introduced in the near future. Can you think what that characteristic might be? It's true of you, it's true of turtles and beetles, it's true of elm trees and mosses, and of all the tiny living organisms too small to see with the naked eye.

Sometimes it is difficult to decide if something is alive. A car driving down the road exchanges gases, and a washing machine needs water. A burning candle uses energy, and a fire gives off waste. A smoke alarm responds to the environment, clouds grow, and the Mint reproduces new dollar bills all the time.

One characteristic, or even three or four, does not qualify an object to join the ranks of the living. In order to qualify as a living organism an object must pass all seven tests.

1. *What is an organism?*

2. *What are the basic needs of all living organisms?*

3. *What functions are performed by all living organisms?*

4. *What is the difference between living, nonliving, and dead?*

Paramecia (pair•uh•ME•see•uh) are one-celled, cigar-shaped organisms. They are members of a large group of tiny organisms called **protists** (PRO•teests). There are over 50,000 different kinds of protists—more kinds than all the reptiles, mammals, amphibians, fish, and birds combined.

We can be fairly certain that the first person to observe paramecia was Antoni van Leeuwenhoek, a Dutch biologist. In the mid-1600s he spent a lot of time looking at things through his simple microscopes. Leeuwenhoek reported tiny objects swimming around in drops of water. He called them animalcules, thinking they were tiny microscopic animals. Protists are not, however, animals. They are single-celled organisms living by themselves.

In plants, individual cells might specialize in making food or moving water. In animals, groups of cells might specialize in getting rid of waste, digesting food, or sensing the environment. In single-celled protists, a single cell must do all of the things that are done by the coordinated efforts of many cells in a plant or animal. Each protist has the ability to respond to its environment, obtain food, exchange gases, get rid of waste, grow, reproduce, and use water.

When you use a microscope at 400x, you can see several kinds of **organelles** inside the paramecium. Organelles are the paramecium's "guts." Each organelle does a specific job to help the paramecium stay alive. You have organs, such as a heart and kidneys, that do specific jobs in your body.

The paramecium has vacuoles and mitochondria.

Paramecia are covered by rows of microscopic hairlike structures called **cilia** (SILL•ee•uh). *Cili* means small hair. Cilia move back and forth in a wavelike motion to move the paramecium through the water. Cilia are short, giving the paramecium a crew-cut look, and so fine

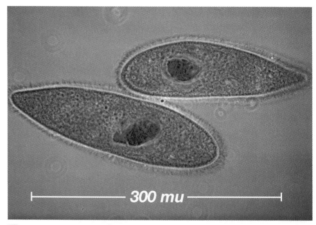
Two paramecia

that they are difficult to see even with a microscope at 400x. Cilia move water around the paramecium. If you watch closely, you might see tiny particles of debris moving in the water close to the paramecium. From this movement you can infer (figure out) that the cilia are moving, even if you cannot see them.

What Holds the Paramecium Together?

When you looked at a paramecium in class, you probably noticed shapes and textures inside the cell. There must be something like skin surrounding the cell keeping the paramecium together. The paramecium's "skin" is called the **cell membrane.** Every cell has one, whether it is a free-living protist or a cell in a larger organism.

The membrane is one of the most important parts of the cell. The membrane defines the cell and keeps the guts on the inside, and everything else on the outside. If the cell membrane breaks, the cell quickly dies. A few materials, like water, oxygen, and carbon dioxide, can pass through the membrane, but most other materials cannot. So how does the paramecium get the food and other nutrients it needs to stay alive? How do they get into the cell?

How Do They Eat?

Single-celled organisms don't have mouths that open to take in food the way animals do. Paramecia do, however, have a place on the membrane, called the **oral groove,** for taking in food. This fold runs most of the length of one side of the cell. When the cilia move back and forth, they swish materials in the water into the oral groove.

If the material is nutritious, the sides of the groove fold over the food and pinch it off in a closed packet called a **food vacuole.** The food vacuole floats around inside the paramecium. When paramecia eat red-dyed yeast, you can see the circular red food vacuoles right through the cell membrane.

The food is broken down by **digestive enzymes** (chemicals that digest food) while it is inside the food vacuole. The digested food moves out

through the walls of the vacuole, making it available to the other parts of the cell for energy and to make new cell parts.

As the food is digested, the food vacuole becomes smaller and smaller. Finally, when the cell has digested all the valuable nutrients from the food, the vacuole moves to the cell membrane, and the leftover waste is dumped out of the cell through the membrane.

The paramecium takes food in and dumps waste out without ever opening the cell wall to expose the inside of the cell to the outside environment.

Paramecia Drink, Too

Cells are constantly taking in water from their surroundings. All cells need a fresh supply of water in order to use energy, repair worn parts, and do all of the other things that have to be done inside the cell. But with water constantly entering the cell,

Water-expelling vesicle before and after eliminating waste.

it would seem in danger of bursting before long. It has to rid itself of extra water.

There are **water-expelling vesicles** inside the paramecium at both ends of the cell. These organelles collect the extra water in the cell, along with some of the waste, and dump it out of the cell. They function very much like the kidneys in your body. You may have seen water-expelling vesicles in the paramecia you studied. They look like little clear circles. They grow larger for several seconds and then suddenly become small again as the water is dumped out through a tiny pore.

Response to the Environment

Paramecia do not have any way to sense light in their surroundings, but they do respond to their surroundings. They swim constantly, searching for food. One of the few times they stop is when they are feeding. They usually avoid very cold or hot areas, or chemicals that would harm them, by swimming away from the danger area. Sometimes their behavior is almost comical. You may have observed them swim straight on until they bump smack into something, then back up, turn, and swim off in another direction. Not altogether graceful, but effective.

Reproduction

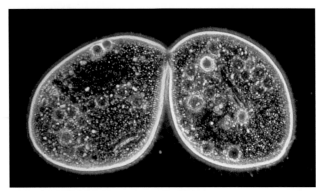

Paramecium reproduction

Most of the time paramecia reproduce by cell division. They grow larger and duplicate all the organelles in the cell. When the cell reaches a certain size, it pinches together in the middle and splits in two, as shown in the figure above. Each new cell is an exact copy of the original,

except half as big. They are called **daughter cells,** and the original is called the mother cell. Even though they are called mother and daughter, they are not females. Unlike most plants and animals, there are no male and female protists, and sexual reproduction happens only occasionally.

The new daughter cells immediately start doing the things all organisms do. They take in food and water and expel waste chemicals and gases. The food provides the energy for life and the building materials to grow. As the paramecia zip through their watery environment, they are constantly responding to food, dangerous chemicals, and high temperatures to improve their chances of survival.

The lives of paramecia and humans are as different as two lives can be. But, as different as we are from these tiny, invisible protists, it is amazing to think about how many ways we are just the same. There are important similarities that tie all organisms on Earth together.

Paramecium Questions

1. *Why is the cell membrane important?*

2. *What are two functions of the cilia?*

3. *What are the functions of the water-expelling vesicle? What would happen to the paramecium if the water-expelling vesicle stopped working?*

4. *What is the evidence that paramecia are living? Give examples of how they do each of the functions of living things.*

CELL: The Basic Unit of Life

One day a long time ago, maybe 3.5 billion years ago, give or take a couple hundred million years, life happened. It was a simple kind of life—a protein membrane wrapped around a small volume of liquid. A primitive **cell** was born.

When Earth formed 4.5 billion years ago, there was no life. About a billion years later life appeared. Since that first single-celled **organism** appeared on Earth 3.5 billion years ago, life has flourished. Today there are tens of millions of different kinds of organisms living here. As different as life-forms are, however, all living things share one important characteristic: **cells.**

Life happens in cells. It did then and it still does today. Every living thing is composed of cells. The simplest organisms are single cells; the most complex organisms are made of billions of living cells working together. No matter how simple or complex an organism is, it is made of cells, and the cells are alive.

WHAT IS A CELL?

Robert Hooke, the first scientist to report observing cells through a microscope, thought he saw a bunch of little rooms. That's what *cell* means: a little room. We know now that they are much more than little rooms. Cells are chemical factories that run on energy (usually from the Sun), take in raw materials, produce chemical products, and discard waste materials. And most amazing of all, cells can replicate themselves. That means they can reproduce an exact copy of themselves that can do all the same kinds of things. A living cell can produce another living cell. Life keeps itself going.

WHERE DID THE FIRST CELL COME FROM?

Where did the first cell come from? Nobody knows, but scientists have ideas. The ancient sea was full of chemicals, and one thing similar chemicals do is stick together. Some scientists think that chemicals called **amino acids** stuck together and formed little spheres, like amino-acid bubbles filled with water. The amino-acid film that formed the bubble was the ancient cell membrane.

After millions of years of refining the composition of the amino-acid bubble, the membrane acquired the ability to gather amino-acid molecules from the environment and incorporate them into the membrane. This allowed the bubble to grow. When the bubble got big, it elongated and formed two bubbles, each with the ability to gather amino acids and grow. At about this point the bubbles became cells, and the first life-forms had appeared on Earth.

Most of the living organisms on Earth today are not much more complex than the first cells. These life-forms, descendants of the first cells, are **bacteria** (singular, bacterium). They make up one of the kingdoms of life, the **Monera** (moe•NER•uh).

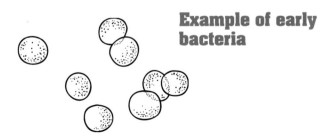

Example of early bacteria

Most bacteria are tiny. They are filled with cell liquid, **cytoplasm** (SY•toe•plaz•um), but don't have organized internal structures. Simple cells with very little organization of the materials inside are called **prokaryotic** (pro•care•ee•AH•tik) **cells.** Prokaryotic cells (bacteria) always live alone as single-celled organisms. Even when the cells of a species of bacteria stick together in masses or strands, they are still living solitary lives.

Example of current bacteria

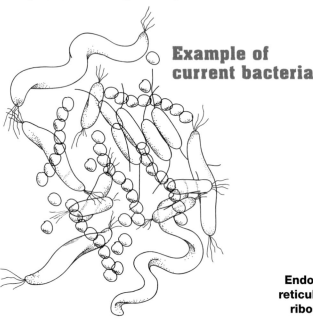

Some bacteria get energy by producing their own food through photosynthesis. Others take up simple chemicals from the environment or discharge substances that dissolve their food source, and then soak up the nutritious chemicals.

This all happens in an aquatic environment. The aquatic environment might be as large as an ocean or lake or as small as the inside of your mouth or the invisible layer of moisture on your skin.

As simple as they are, bacteria are diverse. Some 8000 species have been identified, and they come in a lot of different shapes and designs. Life on Earth would not exist without bacteria.

A CELL WITH A NUCLEUS

Bacteria were the only life-forms on Earth for about 2 billion years. Then, about 1.5 billion years ago, a new kind of cell appeared. This cell had structures *inside* the membrane. Most important was the cell **nucleus,** the director of cellular activities. The new cells, called **eukaryotic** (you•care•ee•AH•tik) **cells,** also had other organized structures in the cytoplasm called **organelles,** including endoplasmic reticulum, mitochondria, chloroplasts, ribosomes, lysosomes, and more.

Protist eukaryotic cell
(Paramecium)

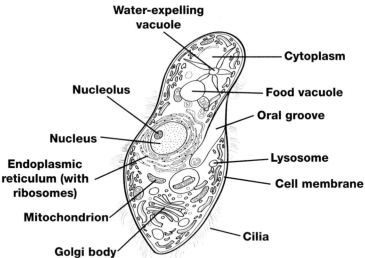

Water-expelling vacuole
Cytoplasm
Nucleolus
Food vacuole
Oral groove
Nucleus
Endoplasmic reticulum (with ribosomes)
Lysosome
Cell membrane
Mitochondrion
Cilia
Golgi body

Each organelle has a specific job to perform for the cell, like capturing energy, releasing energy, manufacturing proteins, or synthesizing energy-rich carbohydrates. These complex cells formed a whole new kingdom of organisms, **Protista.**

Protists were then and still are today mostly single-celled, aquatic organisms. They are larger than bacteria. Often they are fast swimmers, like paramecia, and some are able to feed by engulfing whole bacteria or smaller protists as food, like *amoebae.* Others are able to perform photosynthesis, so they make their own food, like the algae.

Protists are much more complex than bacteria, but like bacteria, they still live bathed in water. Water provides access to food and resources, and a convenient place to get rid of waste. And all of the complex chemical interactions that are essential for life take place in solution. Water equals life.

CELLS INVADE THE LAND

Sometime after protists arrived on the scene 1.5 billion years ago, one group of protists, called algae, began to live together in colonies. Some of the colonies became huge. If there had been any humans around at the time, these colonial algae would have been the first life-forms big enough to see without a microscope. The giant kelps (algae) that grow today in the oceans of the world are examples of this kind of organism.

It was probably a descendant of an ancient colonial alga that first moved onto the land. Scientists think that the first plants colonized dry land about 410 million years ago. Just a short time passed—maybe a few million years—before the first land animals followed. These were some kind of ancient insects. So 400 million years ago Earth had plants and animals living and thriving on dry land. And, of course, the plants and animals

Plant cell (eukaryotic)

Mitochondrion

Endoplasmic reticulum

Nucleus

Nucleolus

Cell wall

Chloroplast

Vacuole

Cell membrane

Mitochondrion

Animal cell (eukaryotic)

were made of cells, and those cells were eukaryotic cells. In fact, all living organisms, with the exception of Monera (bacteria), are made of eukaryotic cells.

AQUATIC LIFE ON DRY LAND

These pioneers on the land had cellular functions that evolved in an aquatic environment. To keep their cells alive, organisms that moved out of the water had to keep their cells wet at all times. That was the secret to leaving the sea: bring a little bit of the sea along when you move onto the dry land.

Algae growing at the ocean's edge today are able to withstand short periods of exposure to air. Every time the tide goes out, the algae living in the intertidal zone are left high and dry. But they are able to stay alive partly because the algae cells have sturdy, waterproof cell walls. The cell wall helps to hold the precious water inside the cell. The ancient plants that invaded the land had cell walls to keep water inside the cells, so that life could leave the sea.

The ancient terrestrial insects probably evolved from aquatic animals with shells on the outside, maybe something like a shrimp shell. The tough shell served to hold in the water that is the key to life.

As life on land diversified and increased in complexity, organisms evolved structures for supplying water to every one of their cells. At the same time all the other needs of the cells had to be satisfied. The cells needed food, oxygen, and waste removal.

When we compare the most ancient life-forms—the bacteria and protists—with the most modern life-forms—plants and animals—it is amazing to think about how much life has changed in 3.5 billion years. But when you compare the *environments of the cells*, it is striking how little life has changed in that period of time. Cells are still aquatic, even in humans. Every cell is bathed in fluid,

and every cell is continually in contact with the blood that pumps through our vessels. In fact, the chemical composition of blood is very similar to that of seawater.

Because we are human, we live very comfortably on dry land as terrestrial organisms. As free-living life-forms we get along just fine as long as our millions of cells work together and stay alive and healthy. One of the most important things we have to do is keep our cells in an aquatic environment. We refresh the water supply by drinking liquids and eating food that contains water. The water goes into the blood, which in turn keeps every cell wet. We are dry-land organisms, but, because life happens in our cells, our cells are aquatic.

1. *What is the difference between prokaryotic cells and eukaryotic cells? Which is the only kingdom of life that is made of prokaryotic cells?*

2. *What features of ancient aquatic organisms made it possible for them to leave the sea and colonize the dry land about 400 million years ago?*

3. *Humans and many other organisms don't live in water. Why might a person make the statement that all life is aquatic?*

4. *Would you say cells, bacteria, algae, plants, or animals are the basic units of life? Explain why you think so.*

Stems and Leaves

hink about walking through a wooded area or a park on a spring or summer day. You are surrounded by plants—trees above, bushes to the side, grass and flowers underfoot. A wonderful display of greenery of all sizes and shapes. At first glance these plants appear to be very different from one another, but on closer examination you will find that they have many things in common.

Just about all plants have **stems.** They may be green and flexible or rigid and covered by rough bark. The stems establish the basic shape of the plant and provide a structure for positioning **leaves.** Leaves come in many shapes, sizes, and colors, particularly shades of green. Each part of every organism, including stems and leaves of plants, helps the plant survive.

STEMS FOR SUPPORT

Microscopic examination of plant cells shows that they all have a cell wall in addition to the cell membrane. The cell wall is made of a rigid but flexible material called **cellulose.** Wood is made out of cellulose. Trees and shrubs that live for many years usually have hard, woody stems called branches and trunks. Plants that live for only part of a year usually have softer, more flexible stems. In either case the rigid cell walls provide the structure that gives plants their characteristic shape and allows them to support the load of leaves that grows on them.

The stems support and position the leaves, so that they receive just the right exposure to sunlight.

Trees in the rain forest that require direct exposure to sunlight need very long stems (trunks) to compete with other Sun-loving plants. Such trees may be over 50 meters tall. Extreme height, however, can be a problem because rain forest soil is very shallow. A tall tree could easily be toppled in a storm. A number of tropical trees have evolved a large bracing structure on their trunks, called a **buttress,** to effectively broaden the base for stability.

Buttressed tree

Smaller plants in a dense forest have other ways of getting their leaves to sunlight. Vines have specialized structures called **tendrils** that allow them to attach to other structures. When a tendril touches an object, it twines tightly around it. As a result the vine can devote more energy to growing long and less energy to building a huge structure. It simply takes advantage of the structure provided by another tree and climbs up to position its leaves in the sunlight.

Other plants don't need soil at all. Instead they grow right on the high branches of established trees. In the rain forest such plants rely on rain to provide the water they need to survive. Many orchids live this way. Plants that live on branches in areas where water is not so readily available have roots that invade the xylem of the host tree's branches and "steal" the water they need. Mistletoe is a plant that does this.

Plants growing on the forest floor have an alternative to long, massive stems. They invest their vital energy in huge leaves. In this way they are able to use much more of the filtered light that makes its way down to the forest floor.

Broad-leafed understory plant

SPECIALIZED STEMS

Plants in the desert face a different problem. Because leaves lose so much water in a dry, hot environment, many desert plants, such as cactus, do not have green leaves. Others, such as the paloverde tree, sprout leaves only for a short time after a rain. How do they carry out photosynthesis and produce the food they need? The stem of the cactus and the trunk and branches of the paloverde tree are green. These stems and branches carry out photosynthesis.

The stems of some plants are adapted to protect the plant. Thorns, bristles, or hairlike coverings are examples of structures that protect plants from

being eaten. Redwood trees have thick, shaggy bark that protects the tree from getting too hot during a forest fire. The bark also contains fire-retardant chemicals so that it is less likely to burn. The stems of some plants, including trees such as cedar, pine, creosote, and redwood, contain chemicals that are poisonous to many insects and fungi so that the stem will not be attacked.

LEAVES

Leaves have been called the energy factories of plants because most of the photosynthesis takes place in them. Most of the cells in leaves contain **chloroplasts** (CLOR•oh•plasts; *chloro* means green; *plast* means formed or molded), which look like tiny green spheres or ovals. They are easily seen in *Elodea* leaves.

PHOTOSYNTHESIS

In land plants, roots and stems bring water to the leaf, and the leaf absorbs carbon dioxide from the air. **Chlorophyll,** a green pigment inside the chloroplasts, captures energy from sunlight. The energy is used to produce carbohydrate (sugar) from water (H_2O) and carbon dioxide (CO_2). This process of creating energy-rich sugar from light, CO_2, and H_2O is **photosynthesis** (*photo* means light; *synthesis* means to put together).

Photosynthesis is one of the most important chemical reactions in life. During photosynthesis, oxygen gas (O_2) is given off by the plant as a waste product. This chemical reaction is written out below.

$$H_2O + CO_2 + Light = Sugar (energy) + O_2$$

FOOD STORAGE

The stored energy in the sugar is used by the plant to grow, repair damaged tissue, and make new structures, such as flowers and seeds. The plant usually makes more sugar than it needs, so some of the sugar is converted into starch and is stored in different parts of the plant. Many plants store food energy in their stems and leaves as well as in their roots.

When animals eat plants, the energy is transferred to the animals. Some plant stems and leaves that humans use for food are celery, cabbage, sugar cane, asparagus, chives, lettuce, and rhubarb. Many animals get their food entirely from the starches and other carbohydrates stored in stems and leaves. These animals are called herbivores and include cows, horses, deer, koalas, and giant pandas. Almost all terrestrial organisms get their energy directly or indirectly from plants.

COORDINATION AT THE CELLULAR LEVEL

For photosynthesis to take place, several types of cells in the leaf have to work together. The drawing of a cross section of a leaf shows many kinds of cells in the leaf. These different cells all have different functions.

Fluids flow through plants in **vascular bundles.** Some cells form **xylem** (ZY•lem), which is a bundle of tubes that brings water and minerals to the cells. Other cells form the **phloem** (FLO•um), the tubes that take sugar to other parts of the plant that need it. **Epidermal** cells at the top and bottom surfaces of the leaf form an outer covering, a little bit like skin. These cells are covered with a waxy layer called the **cuticle.**

Cells just under the surface layers contain chloroplasts to capture sunlight for photosynthesis. Cells in the middle of the leaf have air spaces around them, making this part of the leaf rather spongy. This allows carbon dioxide and oxygen to circulate around the cells. The guard cells open and close the **stomates** to let carbon dioxide, oxygen, and water vapor enter and leave the leaf.

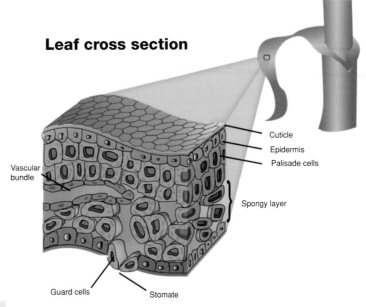

Leaf cross section

Cuticle
Epidermis
Palisade cells
Vascular bundle
Spongy layer
Guard cells
Stomate

RETAINING WATER

All cells in the plant need a supply of sugar produced by photosynthesis to keep growing and building new tissue. For photosynthesis, plants need a lot of carbon dioxide coming in through the stomates and water coming up from the roots. However, water can quickly evaporate from the cells in the leaves. Most of this water vapor is lost through the stomates. The process of water vapor leaving the cells through the stomates is called **transpiration.**

If the cells in the leaf lose too much water, the cells will shrink (a condition we call wilting), chemical reactions in the cells will stop, and if water is not soon restored, the cells will die. Even so, a little bit of wilting can actually benefit a plant when the water supply is low. When the leaf is drooping, it is not in position to capture the maximum amount of sunlight. Reduced sunlight slows the rate of water loss in the leaves.

When the weather is hot, the Sun is shining, a breeze is blowing, and the humidity is low, water evaporates very quickly. In these conditions plants can rapidly lose valuable water. Plants are able to respond to dry conditions to reduce the amount of water lost from their leaves.

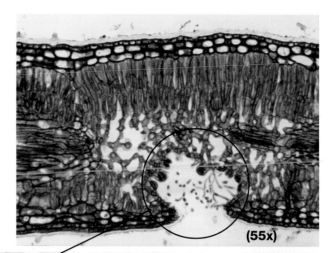

(55x)

WATER CONSERVATION

Fully hydrated (filled with water) guard cells are banana shaped. The curved guard cells hold the stomates open. When the cells in the leaf start to dehydrate, the guard cells lose water and flatten out. The result is that the stomate closes and water loss is reduced significantly.

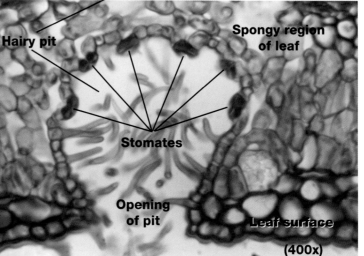

Hairy pit

Spongy region of leaf

Stomates

Opening of pit

Leaf surface

(400x)

Cross sections of oleander leaf

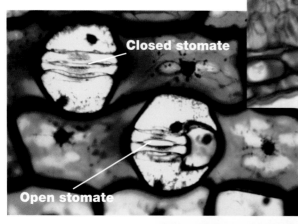

Closed stomate

Open stomate

Some plants have pits in the surfaces of their leaves. The pits are filled with numerous hairlike structures. Stomates are clustered in these pits.

When the stomates are closed, carbon dioxide inside the leaf is quickly used up and the synthesis of sugars stops. For the plant it is more important in the short run to close the stomates to keep enough water in the cells to stay alive than it is to make more sugar.

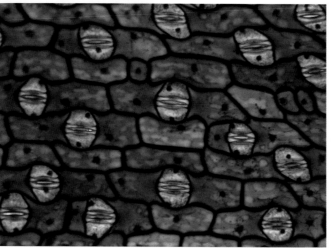

Because the breeze can't blow directly across the stomates, less water transpires from stomates in pits.

Most leaves have more stomates on the bottom surface than on the top surface. This makes sense because the Sun usually heats the top surface of the leaf more than the bottom.

The cuticle, a layer of waxy material on the surface of the leaf, reduces the amount of water that evaporates out of the cells and into the air. In dry climates the cuticle can be very thick.

Some plants have very thick leaves that can hold a lot of water. Because the leaves are so thick, most of the water in the leaf is farther from the surface and the stomates. Many desert plants have small leaves, resulting in less surface for transpiration. However, the small surface also cuts down on photosynthesis. This usually works out fine because sunlight is rarely a problem for desert plants. The paloverde tree and all cacti have chloroplasts in their stems, and photosynthesis occurs there.

One desert plant has a remarkable way of conserving water. The *Fenestraria* plant of South Africa grows underground with only the tips of the leaves above ground. The leaves are very thick, and the center part is packed with water-filled cells. The cells surrounding these water-tank cells contain chloroplasts. The leaves have a clear "window" at the exposed tip. Sunshine passes through the window into the center of the leaf to the underground cells containing the chloroplasts. The cells are protected from being dried out, and they also get plenty of sunlight.

LEAVES THAT COLLECT WATER

Some plants actually collect the water they need. For example, the redwoods along the California and Oregon coast obtain about half their water from the fog that comes off the ocean. The tiny droplets of fog collect on the short, thin needles of the redwood trees and drip off. During one night of heavy fog as much water can drip off a redwood as during a drenching rain. This keeps the trees and the plants under them alive during the summer months when there is little rain, but plenty of fog.

Other plants growing in dry climates have fuzzy leaves that collect moisture from dew. The fuzz increases the surface area of the leaf, creating more area for vapor to condense into liquid water. Dew collected by hairy-leaf plants keeps the soil moister than around plants with smooth leaves.

OTHER SPECIALIZED LEAF ADAPTATIONS

Plants all over the world have leaf adaptations that help them survive and reproduce. Plants growing in windy areas often have slender, flexible leaves to yield to the force of the wind. Trees living in rainy regions often have leaves with points along the margin to speed the flow of water off the leaves. Some plants that grow in cold regions have hairy leaves that fold up around the plant at night, acting like a blanket to hold warmth.

Next time you are in a garden, park, woods, or field, look closely at the leaves on the plants. Compare their size, shape, surface, flexibility, thickness, color, and pattern. They all serve the same basic functions, photosynthesis and water management, but each different leaf performs those functions in a way that contributes to the success of the plant on which it grows.

THINK QUESTIONS

1. What is the main purpose of leaves?

2. List five different adaptations plants have to keep from losing water.

3. What do they do in the grocery store to keep produce from wilting? Why?

4. Explain how humans live on energy from the Sun.

5. Why is coastal fog so important to the plants and animals that live there?

Flowers to Seeds

Why do plants produce flowers? Is it to provide people with something pretty to look at? Or maybe to supply food for bees? Not at all. Flower production serves the best interests of the plant. Flowers are serious business for plants and involve the survival of the species. Flowers are about **reproduction.**

Simple flowers

Flowering plants engage in **sexual reproduction.** This means that a male cell and a female cell must unite to produce a new life—the next generation of that plant—a new baby plant. Although plants achieve this union in a great variety of ways, the story can be generalized.

First a brief tour of the parts of a flower. The most visible and showy parts of a flower are the **petals.** Around the base of

the petals, where the flower attaches to the stem, are some green leaflike structures called **sepals.**

When flowers are starting to develop, the sepals completely enclose the bud. Once the flower opens, the sepals help support the flower on the end of the stem.

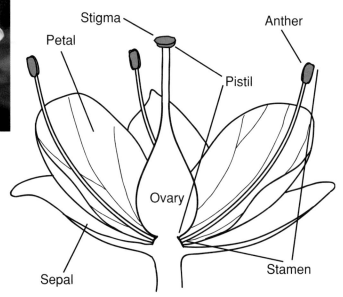

The reproductive parts of the flower are in the middle. Reaching up from the center of the flower are several **stamens**, the male parts of the flower. Each stamen has two parts, the long, thin **filament** that is tipped with an **anther**. The anther is usually orange or yellow. Thousands of **pollen grains** form in the anthers. Inside each pollen grain is the specialized male sex cell, the **sperm**.

Right in the middle of the flower is the **pistil**, the female part of the flower. The flattened tip of the pistil is the **stigma**, and the base of the pistil deep inside the center of the flower is the **ovary**. Inside the ovary are the **ovules**, the "nests" in which the specialized female sex cells, the **eggs**, reside. That's a flower.

Pollination

In order to produce a new plant, a female sex cell (egg) and a male sex cell (sperm) must unite to form a single cell that has information from both of the parent cells. The combined cell is said to be **fertilized**. This single fertilized cell divides and grows, eventually developing into the living embryo of a new free-living plant.

So how do the two sex cells meet and unite? The answer is **pollination**.

Plants don't get around to meet each other. This is potentially a problem when it comes time to reproduce. If a female egg can be fertilized by the pollen on the anthers right there in the flower with her, it's easy to imagine what might happen—a little breeze or a bump might launch a pollen grain in the right direction for pollination to occur. But this doesn't happen in most plants. Eggs can't be pollinated by pollen from the same flower; the pollen must come from another flower on the plant or, in some cases, from a flower on another plant. How do they manage?

They have help. Plants rely on an agent of some kind to carry the pollen from where it is produced to a mature stigma. The two primary agents are wind and animals.

Some plants produce oodles of tiny pollen grains that are easily carried on the wind. That's their strategy for pollination—throw billions of grains into the wind and some are bound to strike pay dirt.

Plants that use wind for pollination tend to have tiny, plain flowers. Grasses are wind pollinators. Have you ever seen grass flowers? Take a look next time you are around a field or unmowed lawn. Grass plants just don't invest much energy in their flowers.

Most flowering plants need assistance from an animal to carry pollen from point *A* to point *B*. Insects do the largest share of the work. Most plants do not, however, wait passively for an insect to happen by. They actively advertise their presence and even bribe insects to transfer pollen. The advertisement is the bright colors, patterns, shapes, and fragrances, and the payoff to insects that respond to the advertisement is sweet nectar and nutritious pollen.

The Honey Bee

The most celebrated of the pollinators is the honey bee. Scientists have determined that bees can see in the ultraviolet range. Humans can't. Flowers that appear yellow or white to us may look blue or violet to bees. Often the ultraviolet color is in the center of the flower, so that the pistil and stamens are positioned right on the bull's-eye as the bee approaches.

The bee sips nectar or gathers pollen, both essential food sources for the bee colony. Because nectar is deep in the center of the flower, the bee has to scramble over and around the pollen-

loaded anthers to get at it. In the process, she gets pollen stuck on her hairy thorax and abdomen.

When the bee flies off to her next stop, she usually looks for a flower of the same kind. When she lands there, once again she will scramble over the stamens and the pistil, leaving pollen grains on the stigma as she does. When pollen is deposited on the sticky stigma, pollination is complete. It's not only honey bees that do this. Many other kinds of bees, and other insects as well, visit flowers for nectar and pollen.

Flower Diversity

The diversity of flowers in the world is the result of the process of evolution. Each flower variation that showed up as a result of chance had to attract a pollinator or the plant that displayed the new flower would not reproduce, and therefore would disappear from the world. Thus each and every flower is adapted to attract one or more pollinators reliably.

Hummingbirds have virtually no sense of smell; they are attracted to brilliant colors. Butterflies often feed only on flowers that are of a similar color to their wings, which helps camouflage the insect. Moths are only active at night. They are attracted to large white flowers adapted to bloom after dark.

Scent is a powerful attractant. Moths can home in on a strong, sweet aroma to find night-blooming flowers. But not all pollinators are drawn to sweet smells. Flies are also important pollinators. Often the odors that attract flies are a far cry from what we think is a floral scent. Some flowers smell like old rotting meat or dung. Such plants fool the flies into acting in their behalf as pollinators. But can you imagine...a bouquet for your sweetie of flowers that smell like...!

The shape and arrangement of petals on a flower add to its appeal to certain pollinators. Butterfly tongues are very long, giving them access to nectar in deep, narrow tube flowers that are not accessible to other insects. Flies have short blunt tongues and more often visit shallow flowers that have small amounts of nectar readily available.

After Pollination

After successful pollination some plants stop putting energy into producing pollen and nectar and maintaining petals. Energy is now directed to the development of seeds. A few flowers change color after pollination. The Texas bluebonnet has a small white spot to direct the bee to the pollen. After pollination the dot turns red, signaling potential pollinators not to come because there is no longer a supply of nectar and pollen.

After successful pollination, fertilization begins. The male sperm cell inside the pollen grain on top of the pistil must fuse (join) with the female egg cell

deep inside the ovary at the base of the flower. Shortly after landing on the sticky stigma, the pollen grain performs an astonishing feat. It grows a long tube, like a root, down the length of the pistil and into the ovule. The sperm, which contains the male's genetic information, travels through the pollen tube into the ovule to fertilize the egg, which contains the female's genetic information.

The story continues. After successful fertilization, the single cell divides, and each of those cells divides, and on and on until the many cells develop into an embryo. Then development stops.

The parent plant supplies the resting embryo with a package of energy-rich food, the future cotyledon, and wraps the whole system in a weatherproof coat. The plant has produced a seed, the living package that will produce the next generation of the plant.

Some plants have flowers that produce a single seed, like a peach flower or a cherry blossom. In this case the ovary contains only one ovule. Other plants, like green beans or apple trees, have flowers with maybe five to fifteen ovules in the ovary, and others, like tomato and watermelon flowers, have hundreds of ovules in the ovary. Each ovule has the potential to produce a new plant if it is fertilized.

At the same time the fertilized ovule is developing into a seed, the ovary that surrounds the seed is developing into a **fruit.** The fruit is any structure that grows around the seeds to ensure the survival and success of the next generation. Familiar examples of fruits include grapes, lemons, cantaloupes, and pears. Scientifically speaking, a number of objects that we often refer to as vegetables are in fact fruits, including tomatoes, squash, beans, cucumbers, olives, peanuts, and eggplants. The general rule is that, if it has seeds, it is a fruit.

Composite Flowers

Composite flowers, such as sunflowers, daisies, and dandelions, have wide, flat faces that are actually hundreds or even thousands of tiny **florets.** Each floret is a complete flower. Many types of insects can pollinate them, and as they move from floret to floret, they track pollen all over the place. An insect can crawl around for a long time, feasting and pollinating at the same time.

Each floret has an ovary with a single ovule, so each floret produces a single seed. The ripe sunflower seed head is a marvel of seed packing. And everyone is familiar with the puffy seed head of the dandelion with a tiny seed attached to each of the windblown parachutes. Next time you give one of those seed heads a puff and watch the delicate seeds fly off, take a look at the bare remains on the end of the stem. You will be able to see the texture on the vacant seed head that indicates where each of the little seeds developed.

Flowers are much more than pretty decorations on plants. Flowers are highly evolved structures designed for one purpose: reproduction. The more attractive it is to a potential pollinator, the more successful the plant will be in the continuing struggle to survive and reproduce.

Thinking about
Plant Reproduction

1. Many plants can be pollinated only by pollen from other plants of the same kind. How does pollen get from one plant to another?

2. What is a pollinator and how might one be attracted to a plant?

3. Why is pollination necessary?

4. Describe how seeds develop as a result of sexual reproduction after pollination.

5. What is a fruit? Give some examples other than those mentioned in the reading.

6. Explain why bees pollinate flowers.

Plants are everywhere around us. Often the types of plants that you see in an area help define a location, such as the majestic redwoods of California, the brilliant foliage of the hardwoods of New England, and the giant saguaro cacti of Arizona. Where did these plants come from?

Once a plant puts down roots, it is anchored for good. It can't move closer to a water source or seek a place with more direct access to sunlight. In the earliest phase of its life, however, a plant *can* move. Most plants grow from seeds, and because seeds are small and self-contained, they easily move from one place to another. During the seed phase of their lives plants expand their range and colonize new territory.

But there is one problem with this plan—seeds don't have legs, fins, or wings. They can't move by themselves. If they are going to establish themselves in a new place, they need an agent to move them.

The process of spreading out from a starting place is called **dispersal.** Young plants often benefit from being some

distance from the parent plant because they don't have to compete with the larger, well-established plant for resources. The methods used by plants to disperse their seeds are called **seed-dispersal strategies,** and the structures on the seeds that allow them to move are **seed-dispersal mechanisms.**

One strategy for seed dispersal is to produce a lot of seeds. Chances are, if a plant produces 10,000 seeds, a few of them will end up some distance from the parent. For instance, the Asian poppy produces immense numbers of small, smooth, round seeds. Most of them fall out of the pod and end up quite close to the parent. Now and then, however, one might fall

Wind-borne seeds

onto something sticky, like a little drop of sap. If a person, dog, or rodent happened to step on the seed, it might stick to a foot for a while and be carried a considerable distance before it fell off. If the new location is suitable for poppies, the plant has succeeded in expanding its range. A 1 in 10,000 chance of survival is not very good odds, but in the long run it works.

Wind

Some plants use a wind-borne strategy to disperse seeds. The seeds are usually very light and frequently have some kind of wind-catching mechanism, such as a sail, tuft, puffball, or parachute. Wind-borne seeds travel until the wind stops, they snag on an obstacle, or they get soaked by rain or dew. Dandelion and milkweed plants produce tufted seeds that can travel for many kilometers before landing. Silver maple seeds come in pairs and look like wings. When a gust of wind shakes them loose from the tree, they fly along on wind currents like a hang glider.

The tumbleweed plant of the southwest United States uses a variation on the wind theme. After producing seeds, the tumbleweed dies and breaks off from its roots. The dead plant is a light, nearly spherical, compact mass of branches and twigs, covered with thousands of seeds. When the wind really starts to blow, the tumbleweed goes bounding and tumbling across the desert or prairie. And, of course, it leaves a trail of seeds in its wake. Seeds that fall in favorable areas can grow and develop into next year's tumbleweed crop.

Water

Plants that grow in or near the water often use floating as their seed-dispersal strategy. Floaters are usually pretty light, with a covering or fruit that is less dense than water. A waxy coating that keeps the fruit watertight often covers them. The coconut palm is the champion when it comes to long-distance dispersal using water. Coconut palms are adapted to grow right on beaches.

The trees may even grow out over the water and drop the fruit directly into the tide. More often the fruits drop on the beach, where they may be washed into the sea later by high tides or storms.

What you see in the grocery store is the coconut seed. It is huge—one of the largest in the world. The fruit of the coconut is even larger and is made of a very low-density fibrous material. A coconut can float on ocean currents for weeks before salt water penetrates the seed and ruins it. If it happens to wash up on a beach before it goes bad, it may germinate.

Many of the plants found on tropical islands were transported this way, and a stroll along the beach will yield a wide variety of floating seeds.

Animals

Animals participate in seed dispersal in many ways. Some plants use the piggyback strategy. Hooks, barbs, coils, and sticky stuff can stick a seed to the fur, feathers, or feet of an animal that chances by. Once attached to an animal, the seed might travel

a few meters or a number of kilometers before it falls off or is scratched free by the carrier. Hitchhikers are usually fairly small and light, and may be sticky like glue (saguaro cactus) or covered with any of a variety of hooks and spikes, such as bur clover, cockleburs, foxtails, and bull thorns.

Want to find out what kind of plants in your neighborhood use this strategy for dispersing seeds? Take an old pair of worn-out wool socks, pull them on over your shoes, and take a short walk through a dry field. Check out the socks after a while. Try to remove the seeds, and you will see how effective some of the dispersal mechanisms are for holding onto a host animal. You might go one step further and plant the old socks under a couple of centimeters of soil, water them, and see what comes up.

48

Another way seeds are dispersed is by animals eating the fruit that contain them. Some seeds pass completely through an animal's digestive tract unharmed. Such seeds have very durable seed coats, such as the black cherry. A magpie might swallow a cherry, fly to the next county while digesting the fruit from around the pit, and rid itself of the seed in a dropping several

kilometers away. Birds and fruit bats have carried seeds between many of the small islands in the tropics in exactly this way.

A third way that animals aid in seed dispersal is by gathering and storing seeds for food. Squirrels are famous for burying acorns, peanuts, and other nuts in many places in preparation for winter. They are equally famous for forgetting where they buried them. These lost or forgotten seeds may sprout and grow when spring arrives.

Ants also gather seeds for food and store them underground for later use. These seeds may also grow if not eaten.

Ejection

Some plants use the heave-ho method for dispersing their seeds. As bean pods dry on the parent plant, the pods twist and become brittle. When completely dry, they suddenly burst, and the beans are thrown away from the parent. The wisteria plant is a champion in this technique, propelling seeds 20 meters (65 feet) or more  with a loud crack as the pods release their stored energy. Mistletoe is a parasitic plant that attaches to a tree limb and draws water from the host. When the seedpods mature, they burst and eject the soft, sticky seed up to 15 meters away. If the seed hits another tree, it will stick and grow into a new mistletoe plant.

Combination

Some plants disperse seeds in more than one way. Beach grass is an example. About half of the seeds will be released to be blown by the wind or carried away by water. The remaining seeds stay on the parent plant. At the end of the growing season, the parent plant dies and is quickly buried in the shifting beach sands. If conditions remain favorable there, the buried seeds will sprout where the parent plant grew the season before. If conditions have changed for the worse, the dispersed seeds may have ended up in a more favorable location for growth.

Back to the opening question...where did all the plants come from? They came from all over. They flew in, some were launched in, others rode in on the backs of animals, some were dropped as the leftovers from someone's supper, and a few might have floated in. Each plant is growing where it is because the plant had some form of seed-dispersal mechanism that worked.

With the successful dispersal of the seed, the new plant thrives, and the life cycle continues.

Think Questions

1. Think about the seeds you found in your school neighborhood. What seed-dispersal strategy was the most common one you observed?

2. Describe the dispersal mechanisms you found on two different seeds. What conditions would have to occur in the area for these mechanisms to result in seed dispersal?

GLIDING THROUGH LIFE: THE SNAIL

What comes to mind first when you hear the word *snail*? Probably you thought about how slowly snails move and the slimy trail they leave behind. And, of course, snails carry that protective shell wherever they go. People who fancy aquariums often keep a few snails in their

tanks, so they automatically think of water snails when the subject comes up. In fact, of the 80,000 or so different kinds of snails (and their relatives the slugs) living on Earth today, only a small minority live on land.

The truth is that most people know very little about snails and seldom pay them any attention...unless they are chomping on garden flowers or vegetables. Snails, like every other creature, have many interesting structures and behaviors that help them survive and do their "job."

Snails are members of a phylum of soft-bodied animals called **mollusks.** Other mollusks include clams, mussels, oysters, squids, and octopuses. None of the mollusks has an internal skeleton. Snails and slugs are very similar, except that slugs do not have shells. Both of them move by gliding along on their **foot,** which is the muscular bottom surface of their bodies. For this reason they are called **gastropods** (*gastro* means stomach or belly, *pod* means foot). If you look closely at the bottom of a snail's foot through a clear plastic cup, you will see the rippling motion of the "belly foot" as the snail glides along.

THE SNAIL'S BODY

Most snails have a spiral **shell.** Because snails are firmly attached to their shell, it is not possible for them to creep out and look for larger quarters. As snails grow, they

continue to enlarge their shells by laying down new shell material around the opening. The shell is made mostly of calcium carbonate, so a snail's diet must include a lot of calcium for new shell.

The land snail has a **head** with a **mouth** and two pairs of **tentacles.** The two larger tentacles are positioned high on the top of its head, looking a bit like horns. These have primitive eyes on their tips. A snail cannot see images with these eyes, the way we do, but can tell whether it is light or dark. These same tentacles also have nerve cells that are sensitive to smells. Like all of the snail's other body parts, the tentacles are made of soft tissue. They can be pulled back into the snail's head completely if they are threatened.

The smaller pair of tentacles is directed downward to sense the ground underfoot for food, evidence of other snails, and the quality of the surface. The many nerve cells in the tentacles and around the edge of the foot are sensitive to touch, textures, and chemicals. Just as with humans, the snail's nervous system allows it to determine what its surroundings are like. When the snail is threatened, it can retract the smaller tentacles into its head as well, and if further harassed, it can pull its whole head and foot completely into its shell for protection.

Land snails breathe by drawing air into a breathing chamber through an **air pore.** The air pore is a small opening on the right front part of the body just behind the head. You can see it when the foot is fully extended from the shell. The breathing chamber is a space inside the body that serves the same function as lungs.

The breathing chamber is lined with blood vessels. Blood in the vessels can get rid of

carbon dioxide and pick up oxygen. The snail's heart pumps the blood to every cell in the snail's body. The cells take oxygen from the blood and give up the waste gas carbon dioxide. If you shine a flashlight through the shell of a snail, you can usually see the pumping heart.

Snails are cold-blooded or **ectothermic** (*ecto* means outside, *therm* means temperature). This means their body temperature is the same temperature as their surroundings. Ectothermic animals tend to slow down and become less active as the temperature goes down. Snails are quite active at 5–30°C (40–85°F).

FEEDING

Land snails will eat a wide variety of leaves, fruit, and other plant material. They are very unpopular with gardeners because the gardener's prized plants are just another meal. The snail's mouth is on the bottom side of its head. It eats by pressing its mouth against the intended meal and scraping the food material to bits with its specialized filelike tongue, called a **radula.** If you use a hand lens to observe a leaf that a snail has been eating, you can often see the scrape marks made by the radula. If you have water snails in an aquarium, you might be able to see the marks on the sides of the aquarium where the snail has scraped off algae with its radula.

Snails don't usually drink plain water, but instead get their water from moisture in the food they eat. Therefore, it is important that snails have fresh plant material, like lettuce, spinach, or carrots, to make sure they get their water.

Snails also need a source of calcium in their diet, so that they can produce new shell material as they grow. Normally they get calcium from the leaves and other plant material they eat, but if the opportunity comes up, they will also eat chalk, egg shells, and sea shells, which contain large amounts of calcium.

When a snail eats, the food goes into its **crop,** where it is ground up. This is the first part of digestion. From there the food passes through the intestines, where nutrients are extracted. Finally the indigestible leftovers pass out the anus. If you feed a snail light-colored food, such as oatmeal, you can look through the skin from the top of the head to see the pieces of food travel from its mouth to its gut.

Calcium love dart

HABITS & HABITATS

Snails leave a trail of mucus wherever they travel. Land snails are most active at night, if a snail's pace can be called active. A typical snail moving at a fast clip can travel only about 6 meters (20 feet) in an hour. Still, even at that rate, a snail can cover 60 meters (200 feet) in an evening. When the Sun comes up, snails head for cover, perhaps under some dead leaves or in some damp, dark nook. In dry weather, a snail might seal itself to a smooth surface with mucus, and wait for the next night.

Snails need a moist environment. If the weather is hot and the ground is dry, the snail may go into a deep resting state called **estivation.** The snail will pull inside its shell and seal the opening to a solid surface with mucus. This sealed chamber will hold moisture and keep the snail isolated from predators, parasites, and diseases. This state is similar to hibernation, but estivation is triggered by dry conditions rather than by cold.

REPRODUCTION

Most land snails are **hermaphroditic,** meaning that each snail is both male and female. Every snail has eggs and sperm. Snails do have to mate, however, because it is not possible for a snail to fertilize its own eggs.

Several species of snails have an interesting mating ritual during which they jab small calcium darts into each other.

The "love darts" can penetrate deeply, sometimes hitting the internal organs. After being darted, the two snails move next to each other and each snail transfers sperm to the other.

After mating, a snail lays up to 100 BB-sized eggs under a leaf or rock, or just under the surface of the soil. Two to four weeks later they hatch, looking like tiny adults. Soon the shell hardens and away they glide, looking for something to eat. Land snails usually live for only a year or two.

Think Questions

1. Why are snails and slugs called gastropods?

2. How many senses do snails have? What are they?

3. What do snails do when they get cold?

4. What do snails do when their habitat gets dry?

5. Discuss the reproductive behavior of snails.

THE INSECT EMPIRE

How many different kinds of insects can you think of? Ten, twenty, thirty? Let's see, there are ants, butterflies, cockroaches, bees, flies...uuuh, grasshoppers, mosquitoes, crickets.

Thirty different insects sounds like a lot, but it's not. There are *millions* of different species of insects. In fact, there are more species of insects in the world than all other kinds of organisms combined! This huge number of species makes insects the most diverse group of organisms on the planet, and they outnumber all the other kinds of *animals* many times over. It has been estimated that there are 200 million insects for every human occupying this planet.

Insects have not invaded the sea, but they definitely rule the land. They are the chief consumers of plants; they are the major predators of plant eaters; they play a major role in recycling dead organisms (ants alone scavenge 90% of the dead organisms in their size class); and they serve as food for countless other animals. Insects play a critical role in pollination. Without insects many plants would die out because they could not reproduce. The diversity of insects is phenomenal.

How did insects become so successful? There are lots of reasons—size, mobility, reproductive potential, and structure, to mention a few. Structure is a good place to start.

INSECT STRUCTURES

Insects are covered head to toe with a tough, rigid, watertight **exoskeleton.** This protective outer covering is the insect's version of the suit of armor a knight might have worn during the Middle Ages. The exoskeleton provides protection for internal organs, anchors the muscles, and keeps the insect from drying out. The exoskeleton is made of a strong, lightweight substance called **chitin** (KY•tin). Chitin is also the base material in horn and is similar to fingernail.

The insect body is always divided into three regions: **head, thorax,** and **abdomen.** The head is the business end, furnished with a mouth, some sensory equipment, and a primitive little insect brain.

The middle region (the thorax) specializes in mobility. This is where insects have their six legs (*always* six) and wings.

The back end is the abdomen, where most of the guts are. These include digestive organs, reproductive organs, and most of the circulatory and respiratory apparatus.

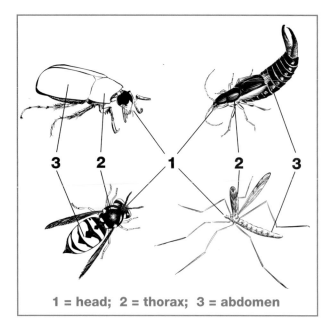

1 = head; 2 = thorax; 3 = abdomen

The three body sections, wings, tough exoskeleton, and especially the six legs are the characteristics that define an insect. It's absolutely amazing what insects have managed to do with these fundamental structures to produce the most diverse collection of animals on Earth!

THE HEAD

Insect mouth parts tell us a lot about the feeding habits of a particular species. They vary widely in shape and function, but all have the same basic parts. They include an upper lip, jaws, a second set of smaller jaws, a tongue, and a lower lip. The mouth can be adapted for chewing (beetle and grasshopper), piercing/sucking (bug and mosquito), sponging (housefly), or siphoning (butterfly and moth).

Another head structure you may have noticed is the **antenna.** Insects always have two antennae, usually positioned near the eyes. These are movable and allow insects to sense odors, vibrations, and other information about

their environment. Antennae come in a huge range of sizes and shapes, and may even differ between male and female of a species.

Eyes provide insects with information about light in the environment. Insects can have two kinds of eyes. You may have seen pictures of the large **compound eyes** located on the sides of the head, which detect color and motion. Flies and bees have well-developed compound eyes. These eyes are made of many small lenses (up to 25,000), each of which sends a message to the brain. The image quality of these compound eyes is not known, but many scientists think that it would be similar to watching a thousand TV screens at once, with each screen showing an image of the object as seen from a slightly different angle.

Housefly—sponging

Skipper—siphoning

Assassin bug—piercing/sucking

Grasshopper—chewing

Insects also have another set of eyes, the **simple eyes.** These eyes register changes in light intensity only. With these simple eyes an insect can detect day length and determine seasons. Day-length information somehow programs insects' bodies to get ready for reproduction, migration, hibernation, and other activities.

THE THORAX

The thorax is divided into three distinct segments. One pair of legs is attached to each segment of the thorax. The wings are attached to the last two segments. Some adult insects may not have wings, or may have only one pair. In some groups of insects (such as beetles) the front pair of wings has evolved into a hard protective covering for the second pair of wings, the thorax, and abdomen. Some insects have ridges on their wings that produce sound when rubbed together. Examples of this behavior include the familiar chirping noise of the cricket and the maddening drone of the cicada.

If you have ever seen a grasshopper jump, an ant scurry across the ground, or a cockroach sprint across the floor, you already know that insects have different types of legs. Insects have legs adapted for springing (grasshopper), running (roach), swimming (water boatman), digging (mole cricket), and grasping (praying mantis).

Insect legs also display marvelous adaptations for specialized activities. Honey bees have bristles on their hindmost legs that hold large wads of pollen, and flies have sticky pads on their feet that allow them to walk up smooth

Hover fly

Horsefly

surfaces like glass. Many insects have uniquely shaped hooks, spines, and bristles on their legs for holding onto twigs and leaves, and for personal grooming. Insects are constantly cleaning their eyes, faces, and antennae to ensure that their sensory tools are in prime condition.

THE ABDOMEN

The abdomen contains the guts of the insect. It is here that you will find the heart, intestines, and reproductive organs. Did you notice that lungs were not mentioned? That is because insects don't have any! Insects have blood, but it doesn't carry oxygen. Insect blood flows around the gut, where it picks up goodies from the digested food. The blood then carries these nutrients to the cells, and carries away waste products.

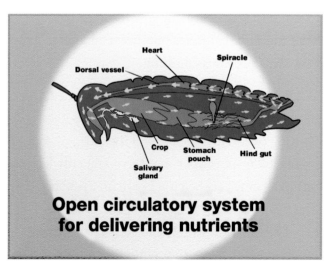
Open circulatory system for delivering nutrients

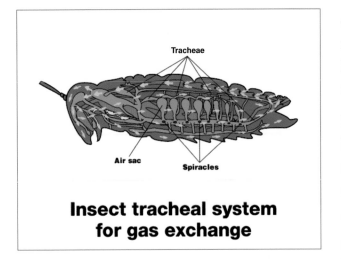

Insect tracheal system for gas exchange

Insect cells get oxygen from a huge network of hollow tubes called **tracheae**. The tracheae branch out to provide oxygen to every cell in an insect's body, and are connected to outside air by openings on the abdomen called **spiracles**. The tracheal system of insects is similar to our circulation system (veins, arteries, and capillaries) in that it serves every cell, but it contains only air. Oxygen enters the cells right through the cell membrane by a process called diffusion. In this same manner carbon dioxide leaves the cell, goes through the tracheae, and out of the insect's body through the spiracles.

INSECTS' GROWTH

As an insect eats, its muscles and organs get bigger. But there is a problem—the insect is encased in its exoskeleton, which cannot expand. The only way an insect can grow is to shed the skin that it has outgrown and get a new one. This process is **molting.**

When the internal signal to molt is sounded, the insect produces a new exoskeleton *under* the existing one. Then the back of the old exoskeleton splits open and the insect crawls out. The new exoskeleton is soft and rubbery. The freshly molted insect pumps up and expands the flexible new exoskeleton. Within a few hours the new armor hardens, and the enlarged insect gets back to its business. The molting process occurs several times during the life of an insect, and stops when the insect reaches its adult stage.

Usually the molting process also changes the body structure of the insect. When the body structure of an insect changes, it is called **metamorphosis.**

There are two types of metamorphosis, complete and incomplete. Insects that develop by **incomplete metamorphosis** have three life stages. The first stage is an **egg.** The second stage is a series of three or more **nymphs** that look pretty much like miniature adults without wings. During this stage each molt produces a larger, more mature nymph. The final molt results in the sexually mature **adult.** Examples of insects that have incomplete

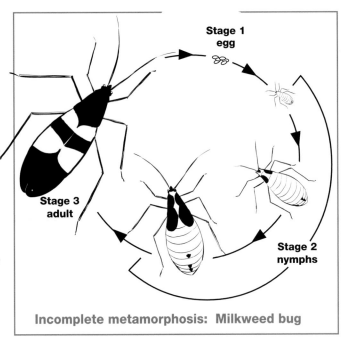

Stage 1
egg

Stage 3
adult

Stage 2
nymphs

Incomplete metamorphosis: Milkweed bug

metamorphosis are grasshoppers, roaches, true bugs, dragonflies, and praying mantises.

Insects like beetles, moths, and butterflies develop differently. These insects undergo **complete metamorphosis.** This is a much more dramatic story. Complete metamorphosis involves four life stages. Once again the insect starts as an **egg.**

When the egg hatches, out comes a **larva.** Larvae don't look at all like the adults that they will eventually become. Larvae are sometimes

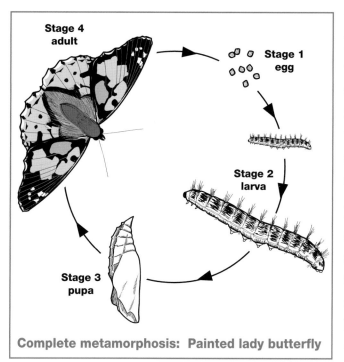

Stage 4 adult

Stage 1 egg

Stage 2 larva

Stage 3 pupa

Complete metamorphosis: Painted lady butterfly

mistakenly called worms, like the larva of the darkling beetle, called the mealworm, or the larva of the wax moth, called the waxworm. Larvae are also called grubs and maggots. Even though the larva does not look very much like what we generally expect an insect to look like, close observation will reveal six legs and simple eyes, putting it in the insect clan.

The larva's mission in life is to eat, grow, and store fat. After several weeks, months, or (rarely) years, an internal signal starts an incredible process. The larva molts one last time and emerges as a **pupa.** The pupa lapses into a period of quiet transformation, often enclosed in a chrysalis or cocoon. During this time the internal structures of the larva literally melt

down and are reassembled into new structures. Often one of the most spectacular changes is the appearance of wings. After a period of days, weeks, or months, the pupa splits and the final molt reveals the **adult**—perhaps a fly, beetle, bee, mosquito, butterfly, or moth. And away flies the sexually mature adult to locate a mate and produce the eggs for a new generation.

Insects are all around us. They have been on this planet for 400 million years, so they have a successful track record. They continue to fascinate scientists with their diversity and their unusual structures and behaviors. In fact there are so many kinds of insects that new species are being found every day!

Because insects are so well adapted to eating our food supplies, clothing, and homes, effective at spreading disease, and armed with weapons to cause us extreme personal pain, we are constantly in conflict with them. It looks, however, like a losing battle. It is unlikely that we will ever manage to do away with the insects that compete for our resources. Insects in many ways rule this planet by controlling many of the systems we depend on for our survival. Without the important jobs insects do, our environment would deteriorate, and along with it the human race.

Those Amazing Insects

There are millions of different kinds of insects, tucked into every imaginable niche on this planet. How can the planet provide a living for so many different kinds? It seems like they would be stepping all over each other. That's not the situation, however. Each insect has some structure or behavior that makes it different from all other insects, and provides it with a unique way to get the resources it needs, find the space it requires, and reproduce its own kind. Some of the structures and behaviors that insects have evolved are really amazing, and there are undoubtedly many more that entomologists (scientists who study insects) have yet to discover.

What's That Sound?

An interesting characteristic that you are surely familiar with by now is the hissing sound made by the Madagascar cockroach. Scientists wondered why these roaches hiss and what advantages they would gain from hissing. Did you notice what moves them to

hiss? Often they let out a hiss when they are harassed by another animal. You may have heard a hiss when you picked one up. But do they hiss at other times?

Scientists noticed that roaches sometimes hiss when there is no threat from another animal. They also observed that males, and only males, hiss in the presence of a female. This led the scientists to think that hissing might be involved in courtship behavior, perhaps used by males to establish their territory or to scare off other males.

Hissing cockroaches produce their hiss by forcing air out of the spiracles on both sides of their fourth segment. In order to test their ideas about hissing and mating behavior, scientists covered up the spiracles on the fourth segment of one male roach and left them open on another male.

Both male roaches were placed in a cage to see which would become the dominant male. The hissing male almost always became the boss.

In other experiments they also found that the male that hissed the loudest almost always drove off the other males. When a hissing and a nonhissing male were in a cage with a female roach that was ready to mate, the male roach that could hiss fought off the roach that couldn't. The hissing male was more likely to mate with the female, and pass on his "hissing" genes. In fact, the females would not mate with a male that couldn't hiss.

Little Drummer Wasp

Humans have been cultivating and storing grain for thousands of years. Insects have been sharing the annual harvest of grain for thousands of years as well. One insect in particular, a type of weevil, chews a tiny hole in a kernel of wheat and lays a single egg inside. When the egg hatches, the weevil larva eats its way into the kernel of wheat and consumes the inside of the kernel until it is hollow. By this time the larva is ready to pupate, and some weeks later the

next generation of weevil emerges. A tidy little lifestyle.

It's never quite that simple, however. Also living in the same area is a tiny wasp whose larva eats the larva of the weevil. The female wasp lays one egg on the outside of a wheat kernel. When the egg hatches, the larva burrows into the kernel and devours the weevil living inside. How does this wasp know which wheat kernels contain weevil larvae when they are sealed inside of the kernel and there are literally millions of kernels to choose from?

The mother wasp crawls around on the outside of the kernels and uses her antennae like drumsticks to beat on the kernels! Just as an empty barrel sounds different than a full barrel when you bang on the outside, a hollow wheat kernel with a weevil inside sounds different to the wasp than a wheat kernel that has not been hollowed out. This curious and effective behavior allows the female wasp to leave her eggs where they stand the highest probability of survival.

It may be that the human behavior of harvesting and storing wheat increases the survival potential of both the weevil and the wasp. Do you see why?

Reproduction Strategies

Aphids are tiny insects that are sometimes considered pests because they literally suck the vitality out of plants. Aphids have mouthparts shaped like a straw that they insert into a plant's phloem and tap the sugar-rich

Female drummer wasp

Adult grain weevils

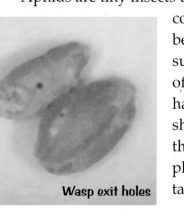

Wasp exit holes

sap. If a large number of aphids descend on a plant, they can weaken or even kill it.

Aphids can reproduce very quickly because they give birth to live, fully developed babies. They do not lay eggs like virtually every other insect, so there is no larval or pupal stage to slow things down. This is almost like being born an adult, except for the fact that newborns are tiny. When an aphid is born, it can begin feeding *and reproducing* almost immediately. Talk about a head start!

Young aphids are clones of their mother, which means that all aphids are female. There are no male aphids. Not only do aphids have **asexual reproduction** (the creation of offspring by a single parent, without the union of a sperm and egg), they have also evolved another strategy for shortening the time between generations. Many aphids are born pregnant. Entomologists have dissected aphids under a microscope and found aphids ready to give birth to baby aphids that also had babies inside of them! It is easy to see how aphids could take over an entire field of plants in just days.

The Big Aphid Roundup

Imagine a life where you never drank water. Instead, every time you were thirsty you reached for a big liter-sized Quenchmaster of your favorite cola and gulped it down. Then you followed it with another and another and another...That's basically the life of an aphid.

If you maintained a diet with that much sugar, your body wouldn't be able to use it all, not to mention the fact you'd be heading for the bathroom every 5 minutes. Where would all the excess sugar go? A good bit of it would probably end up in your urine. That's how your body gets rid of wastes, and in this case, that extra sugar would be a waste product. This same thing happens to aphids.

Instead of drinking cola all day, they drink the sap from plants, which has a large amount of sugar in it. The aphids can't digest it all, so the extra sugar comes out the back of the aphids as a sticky sweet substance called honeydew.

At some point this honeydew came to the attention of a particular kind of ant. In time the ants came to rely on it as their only source of food. They have developed an

Ants herding aphids

amazing way to guarantee a steady supply of honeydew for themselves. They created ranches! The aphids are their stock, and plants with a good supply of sap are their ranges.

Every morning the ants round up the aphids and drive or carry them out to feed on plants. While they are feeding, the ants make sure that the aphids don't wander off or get rustled by an outsider. If a ladybird beetle (a voracious predator that eats six times its own weight in aphids every day) comes by, the ants herd the aphids into small groups and defend their stock from attack. At the end of the day the ants take the aphids back to the anthill,

Female silk moth

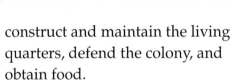
Male silk moth

where they spend the night, and the whole thing happens again the next day.

In exchange for this protection and care from the ants, the aphids have no problem with letting the ants harvest the honeydew for food. This benefits the ants (because they get an easy source of great food) and the aphids (because they get a place to live and protection from predators). If you ever get a chance to watch this happen, you'll be

amazed at how much it resembles cowboys herding cattle on a ranch! Except the ants don't wear boots or holler "Yee-haw."

Pheromones: Insect Calling Cards

Ants are social insects. Social insects live together and rely on each other for survival. They work together to raise the young, construct and maintain the living quarters, defend the colony, and obtain food.

Acquiring food is always a challenge. To locate food the foragers leave the colony and strike out into the environment, looking for something good to eat. They wander out without a plan and without a guidance system. The path they follow is random as they search here and there. If an ant runs across a scrap of seed or a grain of sugar, she will eat it, but her quest is for something good that is way more than she can eat herself. She is foraging for the whole colony.

When she does come across a dead moth, piece of donut, or chunk of cheese, she pries off a crumb and heads back to the nest.

She keeps an antenna to the ground to pick up the faint scent laid down by other ants to guide her home. As she advances toward home, she lowers her abdomen to leave a minute drop of a powerful chemical on the ground. This is a **pheromone,** a chemical message that other ants will follow to relocate the food source.

Back at the nest the ant shows the sample of the prize she has located. The other foragers note the particular pheromone smell of the ant that brought in the food, and follow her smell back to the bounty. The other foragers retrace the path of the first one, each leaving additional pheromone markers on the path. In a short time a wide stream of thousands of ants is hurrying in both directions over the invisible but vividly marked (if you are an ant) trail. Pheromones are very effective agents of communication for ants, both to assist with the business of the colony and to identify intruders from rival colonies.

Trail marking and identification are two ways ants use pheromones. Moths have another use. Because moths are active at night, it's not so easy to find things. And one thing that must be found to ensure the survival of the species is a mate. Moths use a pheromone, or rather, the female moth uses a pheromone. The male responds.

When the time of year is right, the female moth flies out, parks on a tree limb or rock, and starts to advertise her availability by releasing a bit of her irresistible perfume. Any male moth 2 kilometers downwind who happens to encounter a molecule or two of the heavenly scent on his antenna will start to fly toward its source. If he is fortunate enough to find the source he may mate, reinforcing the effectiveness of the scent to bring the male and female moths together.

Every insect has a story to tell about how it survives and reproduces. The stories above are just a few of the astonishing adaptations of insects. There are thousands more. For instance, how do mosquitoes find you in the dark when you are the only person around for miles? Why do moths fly around your porch light? What are the leaf-cutter ants doing underground with all those circles of leaf? Imagine how many more tales there are and how many more natural history stories there will be when scientists are able to study *all* the species of insects!

Think Questions

1. When does a hissing cockroach hiss? How does the hissing benefit the cockroach?

2. The wheat weevil and the drummer wasp may benefit from the activities of humans. Can you think of another insect that may benefit from living around humans? Explain the benefit.

3. If you bother a wasp, you might find yourself pursued by the whole colony. What do you think makes them all so aggressive?

Kingdoms of Life

Earth is populated with millions of different kinds of organisms, all doing their own thing to get what they need to survive and reproduce. Organizing and classifying all this diversity of life is the work of scientists called **taxonomists.** For instance, a taxonomist might start by putting all the plants in one group and all the animals in another. She might then look at all the animals and divide them into smaller groups: the birds here, the insects there, the snakes in another group, and so on. That would be a start.

Over the years the classification system has changed as more and more is learned about life on Earth. And it seems likely that the organization will continue to change. So the system we have today may not be the system of the future.

Today most taxonomists divide organisms into five large categories called **kingdoms.** The organisms in one kingdom are fundamentally different from the organisms in the other kingdoms. The kingdoms are Monera, Protista, Fungi (FUN•jie), Animalia, and Plantae. The two kingdoms of life most familiar to humans are plants and animals. The less well-known kingdoms are Fungi (mushrooms, yeast, mold, and others), Monera (bacteria), and Protista (including organisms like paramecia, seaweed, and pond scum). The unknown kingdoms of life are, however, very important to us in ways we will explore.

Kingdom Monera

Kingdom Monera is recognized as the most primitive of the five kingdoms. All bacteria fall into this kingdom. Bacteria are all

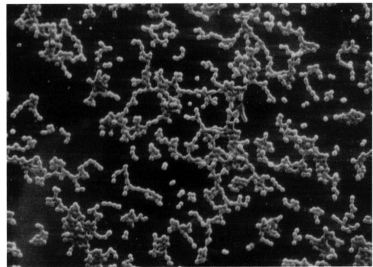

Streptococcous (2700x)

single-celled organisms. Unlike the cells in all other kingdoms, the insides of bacteria are quite simple. They contain no organelles and no nucleus. Bacteria cells are called prokaryotes (*pro* means before and *karyon* means kernel or nucleus). All other living organisms are eukaryotes (*eu* means true) and contain a true nucleus and organelles. The prokaryotic cell is the feature of organisms in kingdom Monera that separates them from all other living things. About 8000 different kinds of bacteria have been identified, and there are probably a lot more to be discovered.

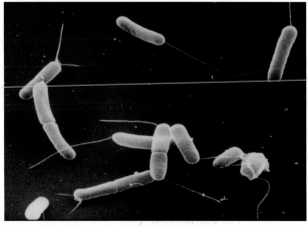

Bacilli with flagella (26,000x)

Scientists have found bacteria fossils in rocks 3.5 billion years old. For the first 2 billion years after their appearance on Earth, they must have existed in huge numbers, because it is suspected that the oxygen in our atmosphere was created as a result of their photosynthetic activities. Before bacteria started putting oxygen into the air, the atmosphere was mostly carbon dioxide and methane, a mix that is toxic to life on Earth today.

Here's something interesting. If you remember the *Jurassic Park* story, you'll recall that scientists extracted dinosaur DNA from dinosaur blood that mosquitoes had sucked up. The mosquitoes with the blood were supposedly trapped in pine pitch and preserved when the pitch was fossilized, turning into amber. That was fiction, but in reality microbiologists at California Polytechnic State University have successfully extracted bacteria from amber and revived them! To date they have brought back to life more than 1200 species of bacteria, some as old as 135 million years.

So Small and So Many

Bacteria are the smallest living organisms. The typical *Escherichia coli* bacterium is only about 2 micrometers (0.000078 inch) across. Bacteria were unknown to science until the 1800s because the powerful microscopes needed to see them had not yet been developed. The *effects* of bacteria were observable, and masses, called colonies or cultures of bacteria, could be seen, but the individual organisms themselves were a mystery.

Bacteria are found in every environment. Some species can survive in boiling hot springs; others are adapted to live in polar ice. Bacteria live in and on our bodies. While some bacteria can cause disease, bad breath, or tooth decay, most are harmless or beneficial to human life. For instance, the community of bacteria and other organisms living in our intestines is necessary for efficient digestion of food.

The metabolic activities of these tiniest organisms are essential to maintaining the ecological balance of the planet. In the process of getting the nutrients they need for life, they decompose dead organic matter into water, gases, and minerals. Although they are small, their numbers make bacteria important in the operation of every ecosystem.

Bacteria can live in air, but only in low concentrations. Water can support large numbers of bacteria; fertile soil, where bacteria decompose organic matter, may contain millions of bacteria per gram; and feces may have concentrations exceeding a billion bacteria per gram. Even though bacteria live in large numbers in streams,

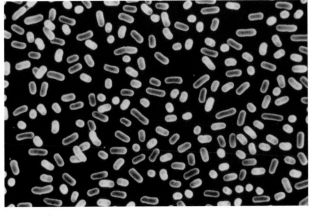

E. coli

rivers, and lakes, their presence is not necessarily a health threat. However, some bacteria, such as *E. coli*, commonly found in the intestinal tract, may indicate contamination and the possible presence of other harmful bacteria. Disease-causing bacteria and microorganisms that promote fermentation are frequently referred to as **microbes.**

Kingdom Protista

Kingdom Protista contains the single-celled organisms studied in Investigation 3. Paramecia, euglenas, and amoebae are examples of single-celled organisms that are capable of performing all the functions of life. Each single-celled protist has the ability to respond to its environment, obtain food, exchange gases, get rid of waste, reproduce, grow, and use water.

Also included in Protista are the algae. Algae are plant-like organisms, most of which

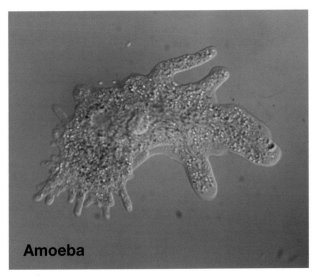

Amoeba

live in water. They contain chloroplasts, and many are multicellular. Algae are the main photosynthesizers in the oceans. They produce the food that is eaten by the animals living in the marine environments that cover nearly 75% of Earth.

This kingdom contains the smallest eukaryotes and some of the longest and fastest growing ones. One type of brown algae, called kelp, can exceed 100 meters in length. Groves of kelp support an abundance of marine life.

Diatoms (unicellular algae) have a silica cell wall—a crystalline glasslike shell. After these marine organisms die, the glassy cell walls form huge deposits on the ocean floor. These deposits are mined as diatomite, a mineral that forms from these deposits. One cubic centimeter of diatomite contains more than 3 million diatom cell walls. When ground into a fine powder, diatomaceous earth can be used for purposes as diverse as the mild abrasive in toothpaste and the thickener in paint.

Kingdom Fungi

The first fungi appeared on Earth about 400 million years ago. Now they are diversified into 75,000 different species, including molds, mildews, yeasts, mushrooms, truffles, rusts, and smuts. Fungi were originally included in the plant kingdom, but we now know they are only superficially similar to plants. They have cell walls, but not chlorophyll, and they don't have familiar plant structures, such as leaves, stems, and roots.

Fungi decompose and consume organic material for nutrition, including dead organisms, leaves, wood, paper, cloth, and leather. The common form of fungus is a unique tissue called mycelium. Mycelium is a mass of tubular filaments (hyphae) hidden in soil, wood, or other organic matter. The part of the fungus we usually see is the fruiting body—mushrooms and the furry, velvety mat that forms on old bread or pieces of pizza lost in the refrigerator. Because one network of underground mycelium can grow to cover many acres, fungi are considered by some scientists to be the largest living organisms in the world.

The importance of fungi as decomposers cannot be overemphasized. Some attack living plants and animals, and others specialize in dead material. Athlete's foot (*Tinea pedis*), toenail fungus (*Tinea unguinum*), ringworm (*Tinea corporis* and *Tinea capitis*), and jock itch (*Tinea cruris*) are all fungi that attack human tissue. When these diseases were first described in the 19th century, it was generally believed that they were caused by worms (*Tinea*). Even after further research revealed that they were fungi, the name stuck.

Fungal diseases are more difficult to treat in humans than bacterial disease. Prokaryotic bacteria can be bombarded with a wide range of drugs and antibiotics that have little effect on the eukaryotic cells of a human host. Fungi are eukaryotes, however, and substances that are toxic to fungi are also toxic to human cells. As a result, treatment of fungal diseases uses very low doses over a long period of time.

There is a particular fungus called ergot that lives on rye grain. If eaten, this mold can cause convulsions, disorientation, miscarriages, and sometimes death. Ergot is also the source of lysergic acid from which LSD (lysergic acid diethylamide) is synthesized. There is evidence that there was an outbreak of ergot contamination in Essex County, Massachusetts, in 1691–1692, coinciding with the hysteria of the Salem witch trials. Putting all this evidence together suggests that the strange behavior of the "witches" may have resulted from eating ergot-contaminated bread.

Bacteria, Algae, and Fungi in Foods

Bacteria are found in many foods, either naturally or introduced to produce a specific quality. Pathogenic (disease-causing) bacteria can also find their way into foods that have not been processed or pasteurized properly. The bacterium *Clostridium botulinum,* which is responsible for the disease botulism, can live in nonacidic canned foods that were not thoroughly cooked before canning. The botulism toxin produces severe and often fatal intestinal dysfunction. Other bacterial infections, such as salmonella, typhoid, and dysentery, are passed along in foods that have been handled by infected food processors.

Most bacteria found in food are added to aid in food production, often as a natural preservative. Bacteria convert milk to buttermilk, cheese, and yogurt. The addition of a variety of bacteria and fungi gives cheeses their distinctive flavors and appearances.

Bacteria and yeast are the keys to pickling and fermentation. As bacteria grow and multiply, they release acid as a waste product. Acid makes foods sour and preserves them against spoilage. As yeasts grow and consume the sugars in their environment, they produce alcohol and carbon dioxide. As bread bakes, the alcohol vaporizes, producing the familiar yeasty aroma. The processing of pickles, sauerkraut, green olives, kimchi, soy sauce, and vinegar would not be possible without the addition of specific microbes.

Food Additives

Algae make good food, and you probably got your share this year, but not in its natural form. These days most algae used as food in the United States comes to us as food additives. Many of the mysterious-sounding ingredients in processed foods come from algae. They are used primarily as emulsifiers, gelling agents, and stabilizers, which keep mixtures mixed and prevent separation of ingredients such as oil and water. They also extend shelf life and improve the feel of processed foods.

Red algae are the source for agar. This jellylike substance is used as an emulsifier. Carrageenan and agar can be found in ice cream, sherbet, jelly and jam, fruit roll-ups, frozen whipped topping, canned meat and fish, chocolate milk, syrup, and creamed soup.

Brown algae are the source of alginates. Alginates give foods a smooth and creamy feel. They are found in pudding, salad dressing, tomato sauce, bakery icing, gravy, sauces, dietetic salad dressing, and milkshake powder.

Diatoms are used mainly during food production. Diatomaceous earth makes excellent filters for beverages, chemicals, oils, sugar, water systems, and antibiotics. You are also likely to encounter diatoms in toothpaste and in silver polish and "nonabrasive" cleaners.

Summing Up Life

That's life on Earth. The diverse characteristics of living organisms have led scientists to organize the millions of species into categories. The five kingdoms of life are a starting point.

- The prokaryotic, single-celled organisms stand in one category, the Monera. They are tiny, ancient in origin, and are represented in every environment on Earth. They are essential decomposers that return raw materials to the environment for recycling to keep the process of life going. Some are photosynthetic; some are not.

- The eukaryotic, mostly single-celled organisms constitute the Protista. They are aquatic. The most massive of the protists are the kelps that grow in coastal temperate seas. Marine algae are the main photosynthetic organisms in Earth's seas.

- The eukaryotic, simple organisms that get nourishment by secreting enzymes that decompose organic matter are the fungi. Most fungi are terrestrial organisms, growing mostly underground and in dead wood and leaf litter. Some live on plant and animal hosts, however, often to the discomfort of the host.

- The multicellular eukaryotic organisms with tough cellulose cell walls and photosynthetic chlorophyll are the plants. Plants dominate terrestrial and some freshwater systems and are the main food producers for terrestrial ecosystems. Among the 266,000 identified plants on Earth are the largest organisms on the planet, the giant sequoia trees of the Sierra Nevada mountains.

- The multicellular, mobile eukaryotic organisms that are in every ecosystem are the animals. Animals have complex internal structures including tissues, organs, and organ systems. Animals are all heterotrophic, meaning that they do not make their own food but eat other organisms to get the food they need. There are more kinds of animals on Earth than all other kinds of organisms put together. Insects are far and away the most numerous of the animals, with millions of different kinds and countless individuals. Human beings are counted among the animals.

When you put it all together, it adds up to an amazing mass of living, interacting organisms. The diversity of life on Earth is stunning. The careful observer who is in touch with the force of life all around will be treated to a new discovery every day. Such awareness helps us all better understand our place in the vast web of life on Earth.

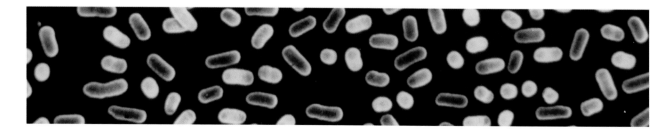

GLOSSARY

abdomen – The third section of the insect body, including the digestive and reproductive organs and most of the circulatory and respiratory systems.

adult – The fully developed and sexually mature stage in an organism's life cycle.

alga (algae, pl.) – Algae are aquatic protists containing chlorophyll. They may be microscopic and unicellular or huge and multicellular.

amoeba (amoebae, pl.) – Amoebae are microscopic, unicellular protists found in decaying organic material at the bottom of bodies of freshwater.

anther – The part of the stamen (at the tip) where pollen is produced.

aquatic – Living or occurring in water.

bacterium (bacteria, pl.) – Microscopic, unicellular organisms that lack a nucleus and organelles (prokaryotic). Bacteria are found in all environments and most are harmless to humans.

cell – The basic unit of life. All organisms are cells or are made of cells.

cell membrane – A semipermeable "skin" surrounding the cell and separating it from its environment.

cell wall – A semirigid structure that surrounds cells of plants, fungi, and bacteria.

chlorophyll – A green pigment in chloroplasts that captures light energy, which is used to make food.

chloroplast – An organelle containing chlorophyll found in plant cells and some protists.

cotyledon – The white, starchy part of a seed. The cotyledon contains food to nourish the embryo during germination.

cilium (cilia, pl.) – Short hairlike structures that propel protists through their fluid environment.

cuticle – A waxy layer on the outside of plant cell walls that reduces water loss through evaporation.

cytoplasm – The fluid portion of a cell's interior. The organelles are suspended in the cytoplasm.

dormant – A state of suspended biological activity. Dormant organisms are alive but inactive.

ectotherm – An animal whose body temperature is the same as its environment.

egg – The female sex cell.

Elodea – Aquatic plant with translucent leaves that grows in freshwater ponds and slow-moving streams throughout North America.

embryo – The early developmental stage of a plant or animal.

energy – The capacity to do work. Most of the energy used by living organisms comes from the Sun.

epidermis – The outermost layer of an organism. In humans it is composed of skin cells. In plants it is the outer layer of cells.

estivate – A dormant or torpid state brought on by hot, dry conditions, similar in some ways to hibernation.

eukaryotic – Cells that contain a nucleus and organelles. All cells, except bacteria, are eukaryotic.

exoskeleton – A rigid outer covering that supports some soft-tissued organisms, such as insects.

fertilization – The union of the nucleus of an egg cell with the nucleus of a sperm cell to produce a cell that will divide to become a new organism of the same type as the parent cells.

flagellum (flagella, pl.) – A whiplike structure that propels protists through water.

focal plane – In a microscope, the focal plane is a flat region parallel to the microscope slide where the image of the specimen is in focus. The focal plane always stays at a specific distance from the objective lens.

food – A substance that provides nutrients for organisms. Photosynthetic organisms produce their own food; all other organisms must consume food. Food is used by organisms for growth, repair, cellular processes, and energy.

fruit – The ripened ovary of a plant containing the seeds.

fungus (fungi, pl.) – One of the five kingdoms of life, fungi are always composed of eukaryotic cells. Fungi, including molds, mushrooms, and yeasts, can be single cell or multicellular. They digest food externally and absorb the nutrient molecules.

gas exchange – Gas exchange is one of the characteristics of all organisms. Gas exchange occurs at the cellular level with carbon dioxide, oxygen, and water vapor being the most common gases exchanged.

gastropod – Snails and slugs are members of this class, which comprises the largest group of animals in phylum Mollusca. The name means belly foot.

germination – The start of growth and development of a seed.

growth – Increase in size of an organism. Growth is characteristic of life.

guard cell – A specialized epidermal plant cell that controls the opening and closing of the stomates, thus regulating transpiration.

habitat – The place where an organism lives and gets what it needs to survive.

hermaphroditic – A condition of an organism that has both male and female sexual reproduction organs, producing both eggs and sperm.

insect – One of the classes of animals in the phylum Arthropoda. Most insects have three body parts (head, thorax, and abdomen), six legs, and antennae.

kingdom – A taxonomic category grouping together all forms of life that share fundamental characteristics. In this course we use the five-kingdom system for categorizing all living things (Monera, Protista, Fungi, Plantae, Animalia.)

larva – The immature, wingless, feeding stage in the life cycle of many insects.

metamorphosis, complete – The life cycle of some insects that progresses from egg, to larva, to pupa, and finally to adult.

metamorphosis, incomplete – The life cycle of some insects that progresses from egg, to a number of nymphal stages, and finally to adult. Different insects have different numbers of nymphal stages.

mitochondrion – A cell organelle that processes sugar, providing energy for the cell and releasing simple chemicals into the cell cytoplasm.

Monera – One of the five kingdoms of life. Organisms in this kingdom are all prokaryotic cells called bacteria.

nucleus – This cell organelle regulates the production of proteins and contains genetic material.

organelle – Structure inside eukaryotic cells that performs specialized functions.

organism – An individual living thing, such as a plant, animal, fungus, bacterium, or protist.

ovary – The part of the plant at the base of the pistil that contains the egg. After fertilization the ovary turns into a fruit.

ovule – The potential seeds found within the ovaries of a plant.

palisade layer – The tightly packed photosynthetic cell found just under the epidermis in many leaves.

paramecium (paramecia, pl.) – A ciliated protist that lives in fresh water and eats other tiny organisms for food.

pheromone – A chemical released by an animal to communicate with or influence another member of the same species.

phloem – The tissue within a plant that transports food made in the leaves to all other parts of the plant.

photosynthesis – The process by which plants, and some protists and bacteria use light energy, carbon dioxide, and water to make sugar.

pistil – A part of a flower. It is the female reproductive structure. It consists of the ovary, containing the seeds, and the stigma.

pollen – The tiny particles that contain the male sex cells. Pollen develops on the anthers. The pollen must be transported to the pistil for fertilization to occur.

pollination – The transfer of male pollen grains from the anther in one flower to the stigma on the female pistil in another flower.

prokaryotic – A primitive kind of cell containing no nucleus or organelles. All prokaryotic cells are organisms called bacteria.

Protista – One of the five kingdoms of life. This very diverse kingdom is made up of eukaryotic cells, most of which are single-celled organisms.

pupa – One of the stages in the life cycle of insects that go through complete metamorphosis. The pupa is a nonfeeding, resting stage.

radula – A tonguelike structure containing rows of teeth in the mouths of most gastropods that is used for eating.

reproduction – The process by which organisms create new individuals of their kind. Some reproduce asexually (without the joining of two cells) and others reproduce sexually (the joining of egg and sperm cells).

response – All organisms are influenced by their environments. The things organisms do when they are influenced by the environment are called responses.

root – The underground part of a plant that functions as an organ to take up water and minerals, store food, and anchor the plant.

root hair – An extension of an epidermal cell near the root tip that takes in water and minerals.

seed – A young plant in a dormant or resting stage, capable of growing into an adult plant.

seed-dispersal mechanism – A structure or feature of a seed that allows it to be transported some distance from a parent plant.

seed-dispersal strategy – A way that seeds can be transported away from the parent plant, such as wind or animals.

sperm – The male sex cell.

spiracle – An opening on the side of an insect that allows for gas exchange (oxygen enters and carbon dioxide exits). The spiracle is connected to the tracheal system.

spongy layer – A ground tissue in plant leaves that contains spaces.

stamen – A part of a flower. It is the male reproductive structure. At the end of the long stamen is the anther where pollen grains form. Inside the pollen grains are the sperm cells.

stigma – The stigma is the tip of the pistil that is often sticky and receives the pollen grain.

stomate – An opening on the surface of a leaf. Carbon dioxide, oxygen, and water vapor pass in and out of the stomates. Guard cells control the opening and closing of the stomates.

sugar – One type of chemical compound produced by plants as a result of photosynthesis. Sugars are sources of energy for living organisms.

taxonomy – The science of classifying organisms based on similarities.

tentacle – A soft sensory appendage used by animals to get information about the environment. Snails have tentacles.

thorax – The middle body part of insects where legs and wings attach.

transpiration – The process by which water flows through plants, entering the roots and exiting the stomates.

vacuole – A fluid-filled membrane in the cytoplasm of plant cells, fungus cells, and protist cells. In protists there are food vacuoles and water vacuoles (contractile vacuoles).

waste – Solids, liquids, or gases that are unusable by the cells of organisms and must be moved outside the cell.

xylem – The vascular system within a plant (made of long connected cells) that transports water and minerals from the roots to the rest of the plant.

yeast – A single-celled fungus.